U.S. Department
of Transportation

**National Highway
Traffic Safety
Administration**

DOT HS 811 381

October 2010

# Frequency of Target Crashes for IntelliDrive Safety Systems

## DISCLAIMER

This publication is distributed by the U.S. Department of Transportation, National Highway Traffic Safety Administration, in the interest of information exchange. The opinions, findings, and conclusions expressed in this publication are those of the authors and not necessarily those of the Department of Transportation or the National Highway Traffic Safety Administration. The United States Government assumes no liability for its contents or use thereof. If trade names, manufacturers' names, or specific products are mentioned, it is because they are considered essential to the object of the publication and should not be construed as an endorsement. The United States Government does not endorse products or manufacturers.

# REPORT DOCUMENTATION PAGE

Form Approved
OMB No. 0704-0188

| 1. AGENCY USE ONLY (Leave blank) | 2. REPORT DATE<br>October 2010 | 3. REPORT TYPE AND DATES COVERED<br>August 2009 – February 2010 |
|---|---|---|

| 4. TITLE AND SUBTITLE<br>Frequency of Target Crashes for IntelliDrive Safety Systems | 5. FUNDING NUMBERS<br>Inter-Agency Agreement<br>HS-60A1<br>DTNH22-09-V-00030 |
|---|---|
| 6. AUTHOR(S)<br>Wassim G. Najm, Jonathan Koopmann, John D. Smith, and John Brewer | |

| 7. PERFORMING ORGANIZATION NAME(S) AND ADDRESS(ES)<br>U.S. Department of Transportation<br>Research and Innovative Technology Administration<br>John A. Volpe National Transportation Systems Center<br>Cambridge, MA 02142 | 8. PERFORMING ORGANIZATION REPORT NUMBER |
|---|---|

| 9. SPONSORING/MONITORING AGENCY NAME(S) AND ADDRESS(ES)<br>John Harding<br>U.S. Department of Transportation<br>National Highway Traffic Safety Administration<br>1200 New Jersey Avenue SE., Washington, DC 20590 | 10. SPONSORING/MONITORING AGENCY REPORT NUMBER<br>DOT HS 811 381 |
|---|---|

**11. SUPPLEMENTARY NOTES**

| 12a. DISTRIBUTION/AVAILABILITY STATEMENT<br>Document is available to the public through the National Technical Information Service<br>www.ntis.gov | 12b. DISTRIBUTION CODE |
|---|---|

**13. ABSTRACT (Maximum 200 words)**

This report estimates the frequency of different crash types that would potentially be addressed by various categories of Intelligent Transportation Systems as part of the IntelliDrive[SM] safety systems program. Crash types include light-vehicle crashes involving at least one light vehicle with gross vehicle weight rating (GVWR) of 10,000 pounds or less, heavy-truck crashes involving at least one heavy truck with GVWR greater than 10,000 pounds, and crashes involving all vehicle types. Crash frequency estimates are based on samples of police-reported crashes from the 2005-2008 General Estimates System crash databases. System categories encompass vehicle-to-vehicle (V2V) communication systems, vehicle-to-infrastructure (V2I) cooperative systems, and combination of V2V and V2I systems. The frequency of target crashes is derived from pre-crash scenarios described in police-reported crashes involving unimpaired drivers. V2V systems potentially address 79 percent of all vehicle target crashes, 81 percent of all light-vehicle target crashes, and 71 percent of all heavy-truck target crashes. V2I systems potentially deal with 26 percent all vehicle target crashes, 27 percent of all light-vehicle target crashes, and 15 percent of all heavy-truck target crashes. Combined V2V and V2I systems potentially address 81 percent all vehicle target crashes, 83 percent of all light-vehicle target crashes, and 72 percent of all heavy-truck target crashes.

| 14. SUBJECT TERMS<br>IntelliDrive, Intelligent Transportation Systems, light vehicles, heavy trucks, vehicle-to-vehicle communications, vehicle-to-infrastructure communications, autonomous vehicle-based systems, police-reported crashes, General Estimates System, and pre-crash scenarios. | 15. NUMBER OF PAGES<br>50 |
|---|---|
| | 16. PRICE CODE |

| 17. SECURITY CLASSIFICATION OF REPORT<br>Unclassified | 18. SECURITY CLASSIFICATION OF THIS PAGE<br>Unclassified | 19. SECURITY CLASSIFICATION OF ABSTRACT<br>Unclassified | 20. LIMITATION OF ABSTRACT |
|---|---|---|---|

Prescr bed by ANSI Std. 239-18
298-102

# TABLE OF CONTENTS

# LIST OF FIGURES

# LIST OF TABLES

# LIST OF ACRONYMS

| | |
|---|---|
| AV | Autonomous Vehicle |
| CAMP | Crash Avoidance Metrics Partnership |
| CICAS | Cooperative Intersection Collision Avoidance Systems |
| GES | General Estimates System |
| GVWR | Gross Vehicle Weight Rating |
| ITS | Intelligent Transportation Systems |
| NASS | National Automotive Sampling System |
| PR | Police Reported |
| VSC-A | Vehicle Safety Communications – Applications |
| U.S. DOT | United States Department of Transportation |
| V2I | Vehicle-to-Infrastructure |
| V2V | Vehicle-to-Vehicle |

# EXECUTIVE SUMMARY

A preliminary analysis was conducted to estimate the annual frequency of crashes that would potentially be addressed by communication-based safety applications as part of the Intelligent Transportation Systems' IntelliDrive[SM] safety systems program. These safety applications incorporate vehicle-to-vehicle communications or vehicle-to-infrastructure cooperation to increase situational awareness and reduce or eliminate crashes through V2V and V2I data transmission that supports driver advisories, driver warnings, and vehicle and/or infrastructure controls. The analysis focused on crash avoidance systems that assist drivers in preventing imminent crashes. Such impending crashes usually arise within a relatively short period of time (e.g., under 10 seconds) from the drivers' encounter with hazardous driving conditions.

This report estimates the annual frequency of three different types of target crashes that might be addressed with V2V and V2I safety applications based on the 2005-2008 General Estimates System crash databases. The three different crash types consist of light-vehicle, heavy-truck, and all-vehicle crashes. Light-vehicle crashes involve at least one light vehicle with gross vehicle weight rating (GVWR) of 10,000 pounds or less. Heavy-truck crashes involve at least one heavy truck, single unit or multiple units, with GVWR over 10,000 pounds. All-vehicle crashes account for all crashes involving all motor vehicle platforms. Target crashes are measured by the number of police-reported crashes in each of these three crash types. This analysis excludes drivers with physiological impairment such as intoxication or drowsiness because such driver conditions are addressed by autonomous vehicle-based countermeasure systems.

The mapping of target crashes to each system category is performed using a set of pre-crash scenarios that describe vehicle movements and critical events prior to the crash. To avoid double counting, target crashes are first determined for a primary system category and the remainder of the crash population is later assigned to the other system category. As a primary countermeasure:

- **V2V systems** potentially address about 4,409,000 police-reported or 79 percent of all-vehicle target crashes, 4,336,000 PR or 81 percent of all light-vehicle target crashes, and 267,000 PR or 71 percent of all heavy-truck target crashes annually.
- **V2I systems** potentially address about 1,465,000 PR or 26 percent of all-vehicle target crashes, 1,431,000 PR or 27 percent of all light-vehicle target crashes, and 55,000 PR or 15 percent of all heavy-truck target crashes annually.
- **Combined V2V and V2I systems** potentially address about 4,503,000 PR or 81 percent of all-vehicle target crashes, 4,417,000 PR or 83 percent of all light-vehicle target crashes, and 272,000 PR or 72 percent of all heavy-truck target crashes annually.

---

*\* IntelliDrive is a servicemark of the U.S. Department of Transportation*

# I. INTRODUCTION

## I.1. Objective

The objective of this report is to estimate the upper limit of annual police-reported crashes that could potentially be addressed with IntelliDrive safety systems based on vehicle-to-vehicle communications or vehicle-to-infrastructure cooperation. This analysis supports the development of V2V and V2I safety applications and the estimation of their safety benefits as described in the United States Department of Transportation's IntelliDrive Program Vehicle-to-Vehicle Safety Application Research Plan [1] and the Intelligent Transportation Systems Strategic Research Plan, 2010-2014. [2] IntelliDrive safety applications will be designed to increase situational awareness and reduce or eliminate crashes through V2V and V2I data transmission that supports driver advisories, driver warnings, and vehicle and/or infrastructure controls.

This report presents the results of a high-level crash analysis that sets the foundation for follow-on detailed crash analyses to define the functional requirements of IntelliDrive safety applications. In addition to the frequency of target crashes, the detailed crash analyses will measure the severity of crashes and will identify crash causes, contributing factors, and circumstances.

## I.2. System Categories

This analysis focuses on crash avoidance systems that assist drivers in preventing imminent crashes. Such impending crashes usually arise within a relatively short period of time (e.g., under 10 seconds) from the drivers' encounter with hazardous driving conditions. These crash avoidance systems increase the situational awareness or warn the driver of crash-imminent situations, and may apply partial automatic vehicle control in support of the driver. Examples of such systems include rear-end crash warning, lane departure warning, red light violation warning, and head-on crash warning systems. Excluded from these system categories are vehicle control systems such as stability control or anti-lock brakes.

IntelliDrive systems are broadly categorized as V2V and V2I systems. They are considered separately and as a combined system in this report. Descriptions of these systems are found in subsequent chapters.

Autonomous vehicle based systems are also considered to evaluate what additional safety enhancements they can effect. Target crashes for AV systems are based on the capability of currently available prototypes or products that incorporate remote sensors such as radar, lidar, and/or camera to detect obstacles and track lane markers. Some AV systems also employ on-board maps and global positioning system to correlate vehicle location and dynamics to the surrounding driving environment. Applicable crashes include rear-end crashes, lane departures, lane change or merge crashes, curve speed or excessive speeding crashes, and stop sign violations. It is assumed that AV systems could potentially address pedestrian, cyclist, and animal crashes as well as loss of control, road departure, and maneuver crashes in which speeding is a contributing factor.

## I.3. Target Crash Types

This report estimates the frequency of three different types of target crashes that would potentially be addressed with V2V and V2I safety applications. Frequency estimates are based on samples of police-reported crashes that involve unimpaired drivers. Moreover, these estimates are derived from statistics of pre-crash scenarios that represent vehicle movements and dynamics as well as the critical event occurring immediately prior to the crash. The three different crash types consist of light-vehicle, heavy-truck, and all-vehicle crashes. Light-vehicle crashes involve at least on light vehicle with GVWR of 10,000 pounds (4,536 kilograms) or less. Light vehicles encompass all passenger cars, vans, minivans, sports utility vehicles, and light pickup trucks. Heavy-truck crashes involve at least on heavy truck with GVWR over 10,000 pounds. Heavy trucks include single-unit and multi-unit heavy trucks. All-vehicle crashes account for all crashes involving all motor vehicle platforms.

This analysis excludes crashes that involve impaired driver conditions such as being drowsy or drunk. Conditions of drowsiness or under the influence may be addressed with vehicle-based systems that alert the driver of his/her condition at any time during driving when the condition is detected. The detection of such conditions may occur whether or not the vehicle is in a crash imminent situation. The focus of this report is on crash-imminent situations where the driver may be able to take an evasive action in response to a system alert (e.g., braking or steering). If alerted to a drowsy condition, the driver may choose to slow down and pull over to the side of the road. Moreover, this analysis assumes that the crash warning system concepts only alert the driver or vehicle of interest such as the following vehicle in rear-end pre-crash scenarios, the vehicle making a lane change in lane change pre-crash scenarios, or the driver violating the traffic control device in red light running.

## I.4. Crash Data Sources

Target crashes are derived from the National Automotive Sampling System (NASS) General Estimates System national crash database. [3] This database was selected for this analysis because it contains the pre-crash variables needed to identify pre-crash scenarios. This database estimates the national crash population each year based on a weighted sample of about 55,000 police-reported crash cases that include all vehicle types and injury levels. This analysis calculates the average annual number of crashes based on the yearly crashes over a four-year period using the 2005-2008 GES datasets. It should be noted that these crash estimates do not account for crashes that are not reported to the police. The national estimates produced from the GES data may differ from the true population values because they are based on a probability sample of police-reported crashes rather than a census of all crashes. Thus, this report provides the target crash estimates along with the 95 percent confidence intervals for each estimate. Figure 1 provides the estimated annual number of crashes by vehicle involvement. It should be noted that the light-vehicle and heavy-truck crashes are not mutually exclusive. Moreover, this analysis used imputed GES variables where available.

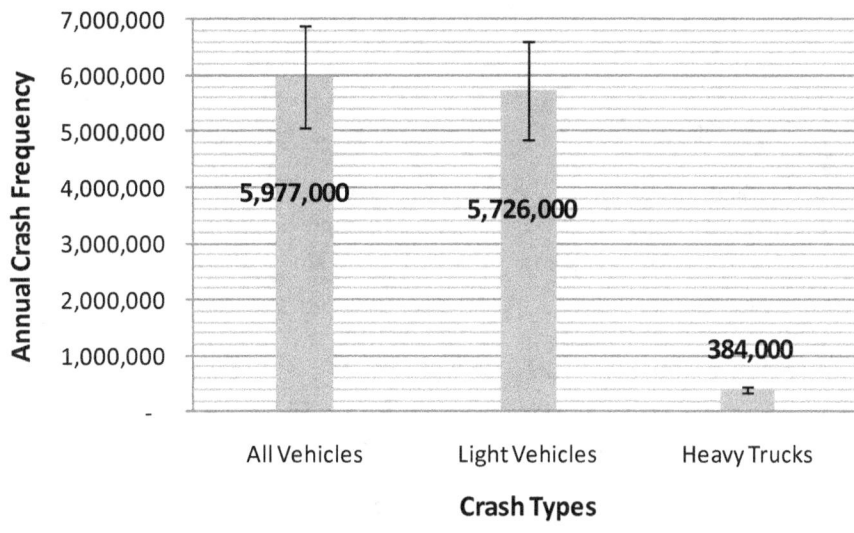

**Figure 1.** Estimated Annual Crashes by Vehicle Involvement (2005-2008 GES)

### I.5. General Description of Target Crashes

The system categories encompass any crash countermeasure that assists drivers without any physiological impairment such as intoxication or drowsiness. As indicated earlier in this report, these impairments can potentially be addressed with autonomous vehicle-based systems that would prevent a drunk driver from starting the vehicle or would alert a drowsy driver of his or her condition to pull over. Thus, this report quantifies target crashes that only involve unimpaired drivers. Table 1 shows the distribution of police-reported crashes in the three crash types by driver condition based on 2005-2008 GES statistics. Figure 2 presents estimates of the annual number of police-reported crashes involving unimpaired drivers by vehicle involvement.

**Table 1.** Distribution of Crashes by Driver Condition

| Impairment | Light Vehicles | Heavy Trucks | All Vehicles |
|---|---|---|---|
| Unimpaired | 93% | 98% | 93% |
| Alcohol | 5% | 1% | 5% |
| Drowsy | 2% | 1% | 2% |

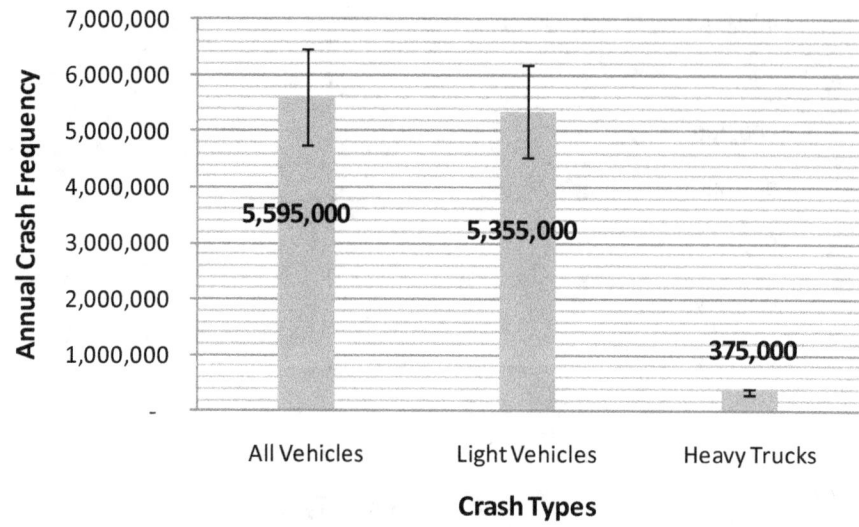

**Figure 2.** Estimated Annual Crashes of Unimpaired Drivers by Vehicle Involvement
(2005-2008 GES)

The following sections of this report estimate the annual number of police-reported crashes that might be applicable to V2V, V2I, and combined V2V-V2I system categories, respectively. Target crashes are measured by the number of police-reported crashes in each of the three crash types: all vehicles, light vehicles, and heavy trucks. The mapping of target crashes to each system category is performed using a set of pre-crash scenarios that describe vehicle movements and critical events prior to the crash. [4] To avoid double counting, target crashes are first determined for a primary system category and the remainder of the crash population is later assigned to the other two system categories. Thus, different analyses are conducted for each system category as the primary countermeasure.

## II. VEHICLE-TO-VEHICLE SAFETY SYSTEMS

### II.1. V2V System Description

Wireless technologies are rapidly evolving, which provides the opportunity to utilize these technologies in support of advanced vehicle safety applications. New dedicated short range communications at 5.9 GHz offer the potential to support low latency wireless data communications between vehicles, and between vehicles and infrastructure. These low latency data communications within the immediate vicinity of a vehicle potentially enable a large number of vehicle safety applications. [5] V2V systems require two equipped vehicles in communication with each other to be operational. Thus, V2V systems predominantly apply to crashes that involve vehicle-to-vehicle pre-crash scenarios. The exception to that is the broadcast of control loss message in the single-vehicle control loss pre-crash scenarios. This analysis adopts the control loss warning function under investigation by the Crash Avoidance Metrics Partnership in the Vehicle Safety Communications – Applications. [6]

The Vehicle Safety Communications Project - Final Report describes V2V safety applications that include cooperative forward collision warning, emergency electronic brake lights, lane change warning, blind spot warning, highway merge assistant, cooperative collision warning, road condition warning, and stop sign movement assistance, among others. Table A1 in Appendix A lists the different criteria used to map applicable crash data to V2V systems as the primary countermeasure and the remaining crashes to V2I and AV systems.

### II.2. V2V Systems as Primary Countermeasure in All-Vehicle Crashes

V2V systems potentially address about 4,409,000 police-reported crashes annually, with the 95 percent confidence interval between 3,752,000 and 5,066,000. If considered as the primary countermeasure, V2V systems deal with 74 percent of all crashes involving all vehicle types. Excluding drivers impaired by alcohol or drowsiness, these systems potentially address 79 percent of all-vehicle crashes involving unimpaired drivers as shown in Figure 3. About 4 percent of the crashes are classified as "Not Addressed" because they were not assigned to any crash countermeasure. The remaining 17 percent of the crashes can potentially be addressed by either V2I or AV systems or both. Figure 4 presents the annual target crash data and the 95 percent confidence intervals for each system category given V2V as the primary countermeasure. Table B1 in Appendix B lists the annual number of target all-vehicle crashes for each pre-crash scenario addressed by V2V as the primary countermeasure, as well as the annual number of remaining all-vehicle crashes tackled by V2I or AV system categories.

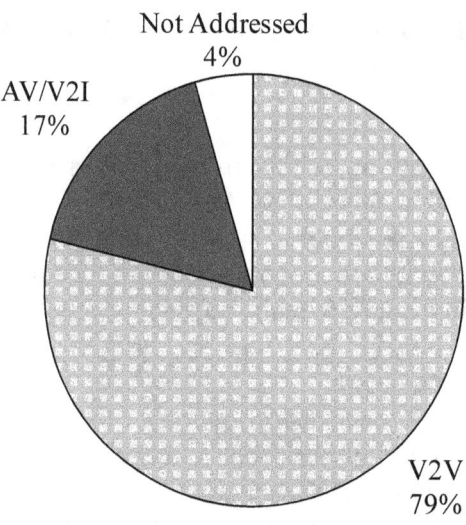

**Figure 3.** Distribution of Unimpaired All-Vehicle Crashes by System, V2V as Primary Countermeasure

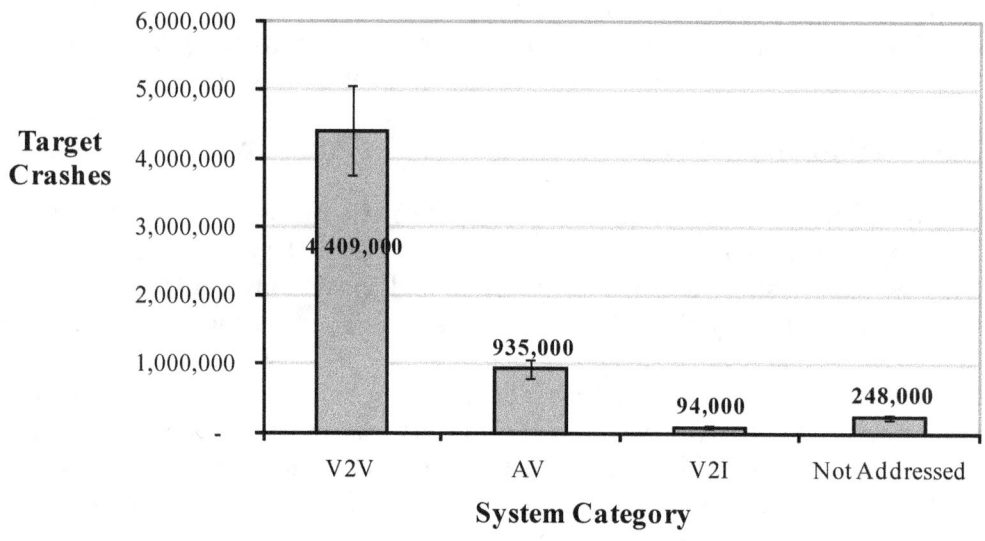

**Figure 4.** Annual Target All-Vehicle Crashes by System, V2V as Primary Countermeasure

## II.3. V2V Systems as Primary Countermeasure in Light-Vehicle Crashes

V2V systems potentially address about 4,336,000 police-reported light-vehicle crashes annually, with the 95 percent confidence interval between 3,691,000 and 4,981,000. If considered as the primary countermeasure, V2V systems deal with 76 percent of all crashes involving at least one light vehicle. Excluding drivers impaired by alcohol or drowsiness, these systems potentially address 81 percent of all light-vehicle crashes involving unimpaired drivers as shown in Figure 5. About 3 percent of the crashes are classified as "Not Addressed" because they were not assigned

6

to any crash countermeasure. The remaining 16 percent of the light-vehicle crashes can potentially be addressed by either V2I or autonomous systems or both. Figure 6 presents the annual target crash data and the 95 percent confidence intervals for each system category given V2V as the primary countermeasure. Table B2 in Appendix B lists the annual number of target light-vehicle crashes for each pre-crash scenario addressed by V2V as the primary countermeasure, as well as the annual number of remaining light-vehicle crashes tackled by V2I or AV system categories.

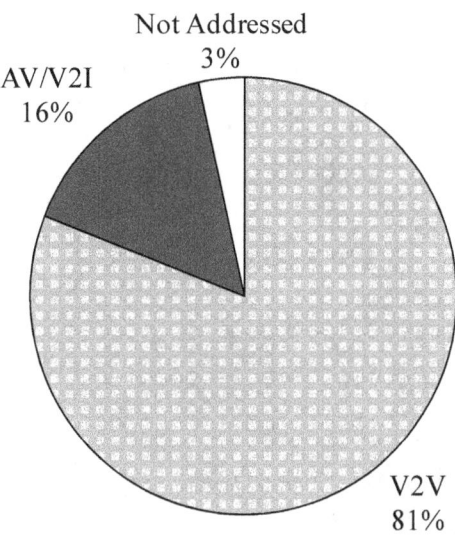

**Figure 5.** Distribution of Unimpaired Light-Vehicle Crashes by System, V2V as Primary Countermeasure

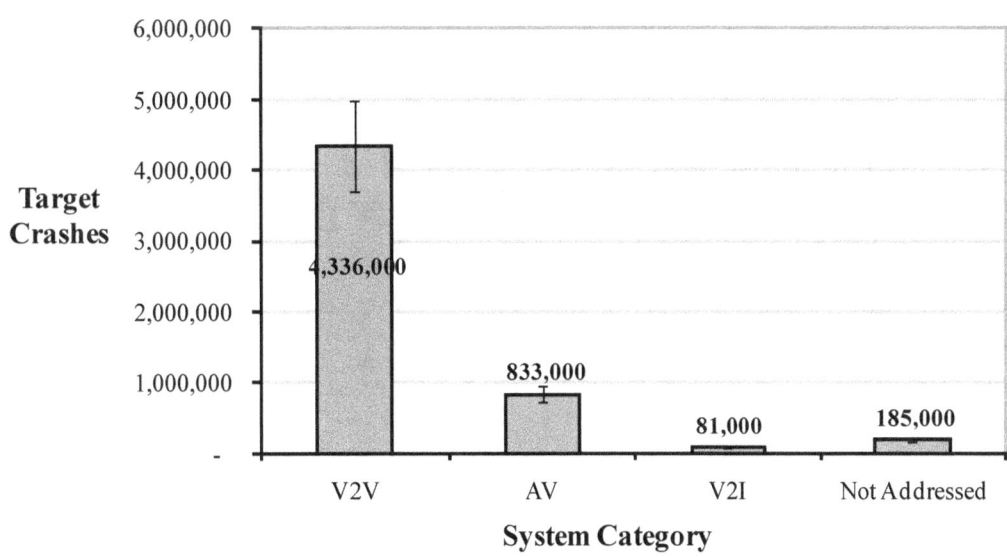

**Figure 6.** Annual Target Light-Vehicle Crashes by System, V2V as Primary Countermeasure

**II.4. V2V Systems as Primary Countermeasure in Heavy-Truck Crashes**

V2V systems potentially address about 267,000 police-reported heavy-truck crashes annually, with the 95 percent confidence interval between 228,000 and 306,000. If considered as the primary countermeasure, V2V systems deal with 70 percent of all crashes involving at least one heavy truck. Excluding drivers impaired by alcohol or drowsiness, these systems potentially address 71 percent of all heavy-truck crashes involving unimpaired drivers as shown in Figure 7. About 14 percent of the crashes are classified as "Not Addressed" because they were not assigned to any crash countermeasure. The remaining 15 percent of the heavy-truck crashes can potentially be addressed by either V2I or autonomous systems or both. Figure 8 presents the annual target crash data and the 95 percent confidence intervals for each system category given V2V as the primary countermeasure. Table B3 in Appendix B lists the annual number of target heavy-truck crashes for each pre-crash scenario addressed by V2V as the primary countermeasure, as well as the annual number of remaining heavy-truck crashes tackled by V2I or AV system categories.

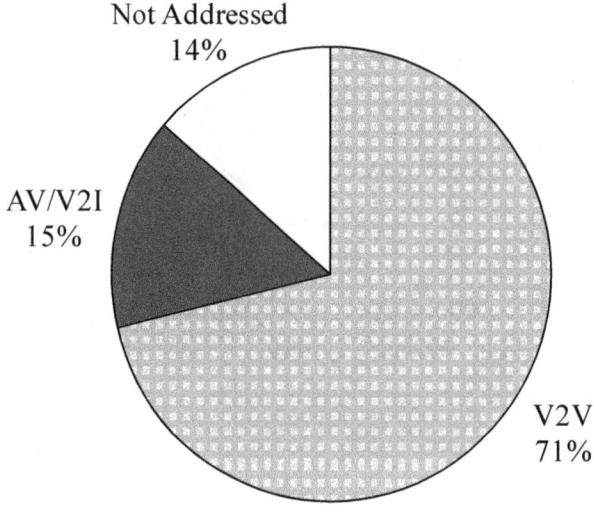

**Figure 7.** Distribution of Unimpaired Heavy-Truck Crashes by System,
V2V as Primary Countermeasure

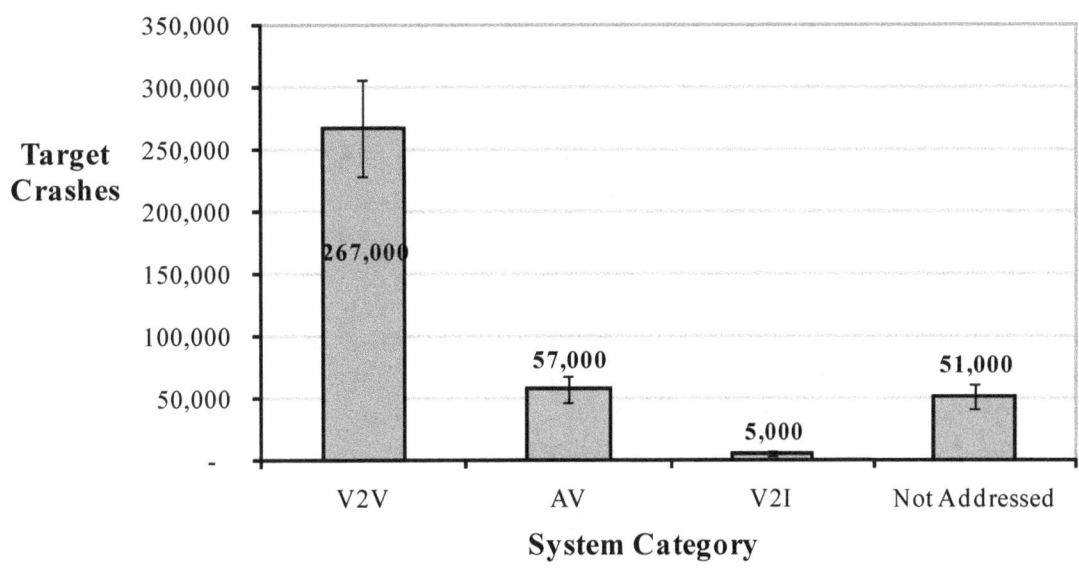

**Figure 8.** Annual Target Heavy-Truck Crashes by System, V2V as Primary Countermeasure

## III. VEHICLE-TO-INFRASTRUCTURE SAFETY SYSTEMS

### III.1. V2I System Description

V2I systems incorporate communications between the vehicle and the infrastructure. Such systems apply to crashes where information from the infrastructure is needed such as presence of stop sign, signal status, speed limit, surface condition, and pedestrian crosswalks. In addition, V2I systems potentially address all crossing path crashes at intersections including systems developed under the Cooperative Intersection Collision Avoidance Systems initiative. [7] For instance, V2I systems deal with crossing path pre-crash scenarios at signalized junctions, violations of red light or stop sign, and pedestrian crashes in crosswalks. Moreover, V2I systems are assumed to assist drivers in crashes where speeding is cited as a contributing factor such as loss of control, road departure, rollover, and object contacted pre-crash scenarios.

The Cooperative Intersection Collision Avoidance Systems Web site describes several V2I safety applications that encompass traffic signal violation warning, stop sign violation warning, left turn assistant, intersection collision warning, blind merge warning, pedestrian crossing information at designated intersections, and curve speed warning. Table A2 in Appendix A shows the different criteria used to map applicable crash data to V2I systems as the primary countermeasure and the remaining crashes to V2V and AV systems.

### III.2. V2I Systems as Primary Countermeasure in All-Vehicle Crashes

V2I systems target about 1,465,000 police-reported crashes annually, with the 95 percent confidence interval between 1,263,000 and 1,667,000. If considered as the primary countermeasure, V2I systems potentially address about 25 percent of all crashes involving all vehicle types. Excluding drivers impaired by alcohol or drowsiness, these systems deal with 26 percent of all crashes involving unimpaired drivers, as illustrated in Figure 9. About 4 percent of the crashes are classified as "Not Addressed." The remaining 70 percent of the crashes can potentially be addressed by either V2V or autonomous systems or both. Figure 10 illustrates the annual target crash data and the 95 percent confidence intervals for each system category given V2I as the primary countermeasure. Table C1 in Appendix C lists the annual number of target all-vehicle crashes for each pre-crash scenario addressed by V2I as the primary countermeasure, as well as the annual number of remaining all-vehicle crashes tackled by V2V or AV system categories.

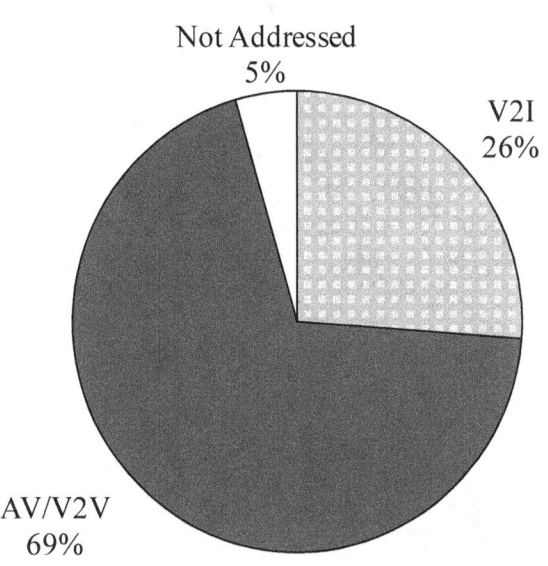

**Figure 9.** Distribution of Unimpaired All-Vehicle Crashes by System, V2I as Primary Countermeasure

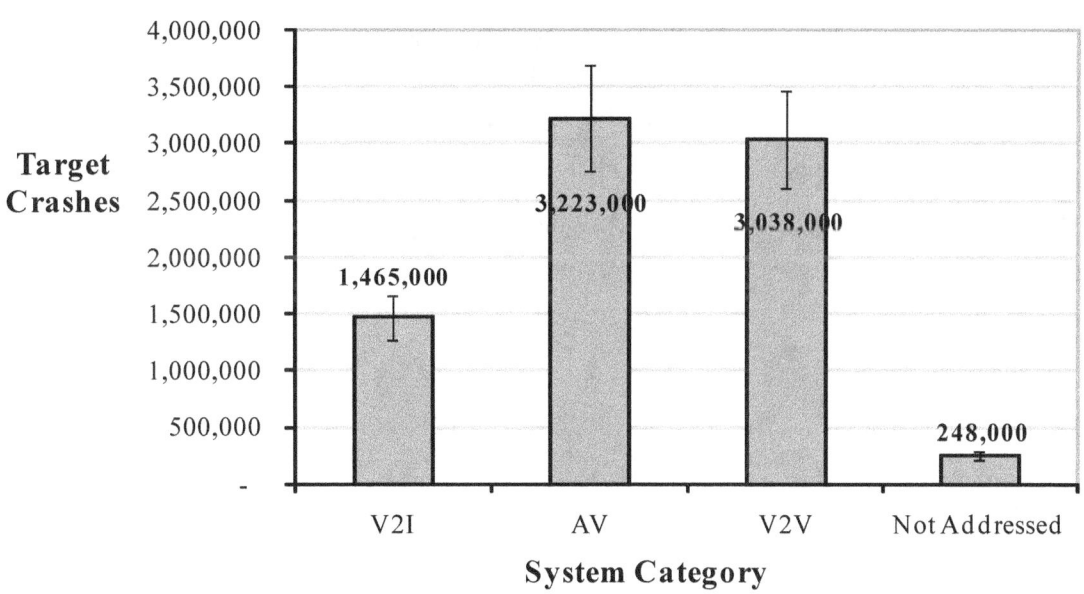

**Figure 10.** Annual Target All-Vehicle Crashes by System, V2I as Primary Countermeasure

### III.3. V2I Systems as Primary Countermeasure in Light-Vehicle Crashes

V2I systems target about 1,431,000 police-reported light-vehicle crashes annually, with the 95 percent confidence interval between 1,234,000 and 1,628,000. If considered as the primary countermeasure, V2I systems potentially address about 25 percent of all crashes involving at

11

least one light vehicle. Excluding drivers impaired by alcohol or drowsiness, these systems deal with 27 percent of all light-vehicle crashes involving unimpaired drivers, as illustrated in Figure 11. About 3 percent of the crashes are classified as "Not Addressed." The remaining 70 percent of the light-vehicle crashes can potentially be addressed by either V2V or autonomous systems, or both. Figure 12 illustrates the annual target crash data and the 95 percent confidence intervals for each system category given V2I as the primary countermeasure. Table C2 in Appendix C lists the annual number of target light-vehicle crashes for each pre-crash scenario addressed by V2I as the primary countermeasure, as well as the annual number of remaining light-vehicle crashes tackled by V2V or AV system categories.

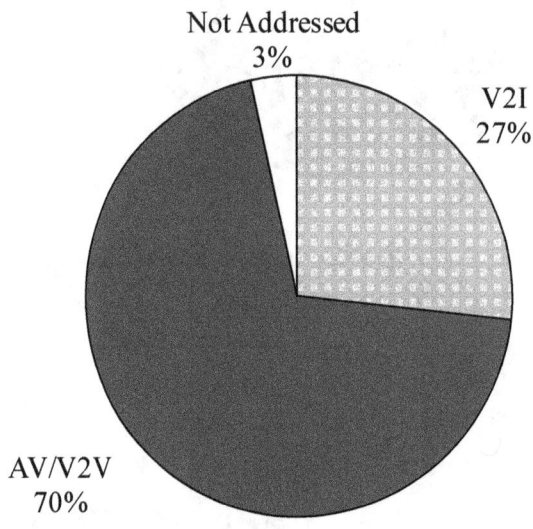

**Figure 11.** Distribution of Unimpaired Light-Vehicle Crashes by System, V2I as Primary Countermeasure

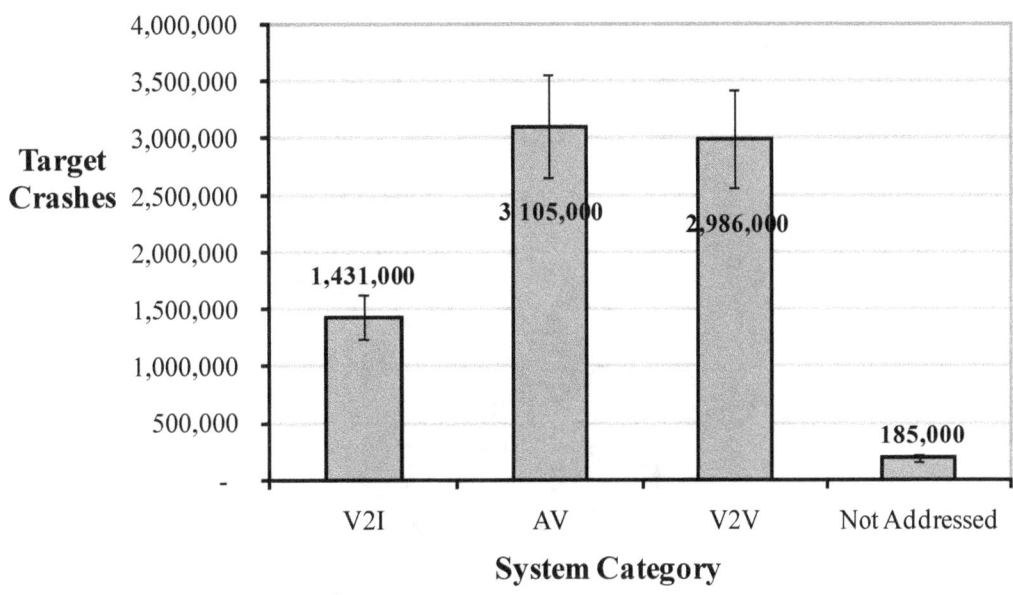

**Figure 12.** Annual Target Light-Vehicle Crashes by System, V2I as Primary Countermeasure

### III.4. V2I Systems as Primary Countermeasure in Heavy-Truck Crashes

V2I systems target about 55,000 police-reported heavy-truck crashes annually, with the 95 percent confidence interval between 45,000 and 65,000. If considered as the primary countermeasure, V2I systems potentially address about 14 percent of all crashes involving at least one heavy truck. Excluding drivers impaired by alcohol or drowsiness, these systems deal with 15 percent of all heavy-truck crashes involving unimpaired drivers as illustrated in Figure 13. About 13 percent of the crashes are classified as "Not Addressed." The remaining 72 percent of the heavy-truck crashes can potentially be addressed by either V2V or autonomous systems or both. Figure 14 illustrates the annual target crash data and the 95 percent confidence intervals for each system category given V2I as the primary countermeasure. Table C3 in Appendix C lists the annual number of target heavy-truck crashes for each pre-crash scenario addressed by V2I as the primary countermeasure, as well as the annual number of remaining heavy-truck crashes tackled by V2V or AV system categories.

13

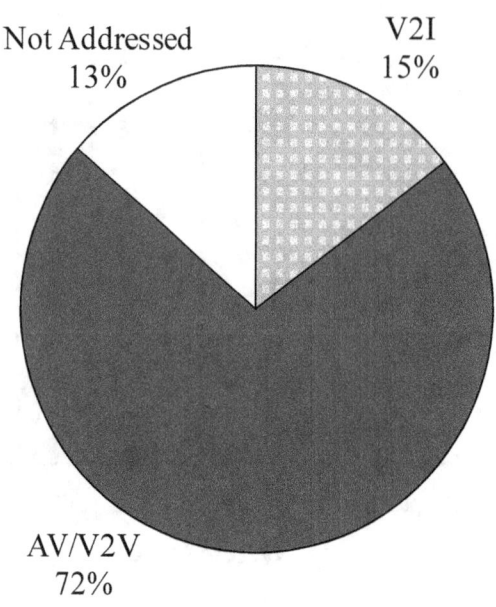

**Figure 13.** Distribution of Unimpaired Heavy-Truck Crashes by System, V2I as Primary Countermeasure

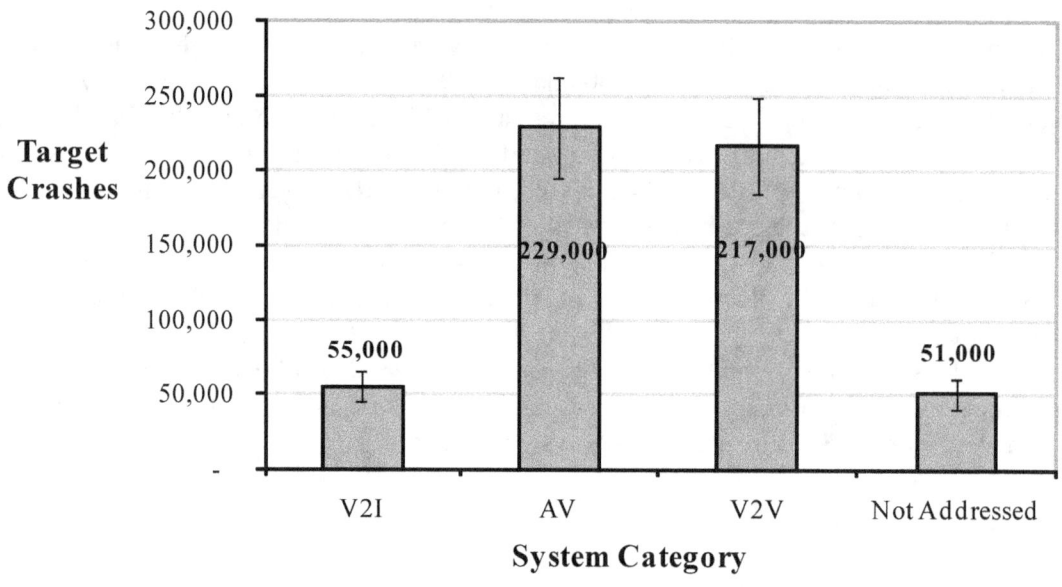

**Figure 14.** Annual Target Heavy-Truck Crashes by System, V2I as Primary Countermeasure

## IV. COMBINED V2V AND V2I SYSTEMS

The combination of V2V and V2I system categories has the potential to intervene in a greater number of crashes. Table A3 in Appendix A shows the different criteria used to map applicable crash data to combined V2V and V2I systems as the primary countermeasure and the remaining crashes to AV systems.

### IV.1. Combined V2V and V2I Systems as Primary Countermeasure in All-Vehicle Crashes

Combined V2V and V2I systems potentially address about 4,503,000 police-reported crashes annually, with the 95 percent confidence interval between 3,831,000 and 5,175,000. If considered as the primary countermeasure, these combined systems potentially address about 75 percent of all crashes involving all vehicle types. Excluding drivers impaired by alcohol or drowsiness, these systems deal with 81 percent of all-vehicle crashes involving unimpaired drivers as shown in Figure 15. Figure 16 presents the annual target crash data and the 95 percent confidence intervals for each system category given combined V2V and V2I as the primary countermeasure. Table D1 in Appendix D lists the annual number of target all-vehicle crashes for each pre-crash scenario addressed by combined V2V and V2I systems as the primary countermeasure, as well as the annual number of remaining all-vehicle crashes tackled by AV systems.

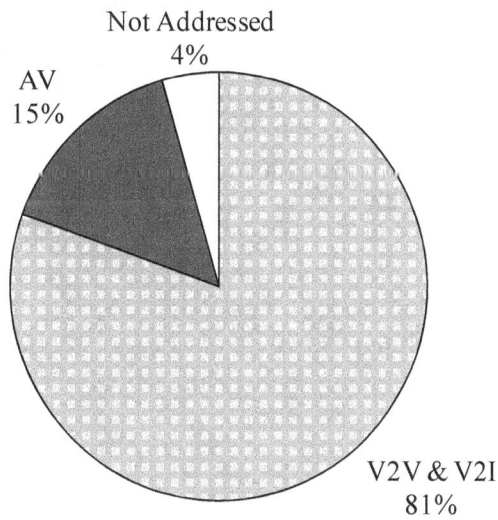

**Figure 15.** Distribution of Unimpaired All-Vehicle Crashes by System, Combined V2V and V2I Systems as Primary Countermeasure

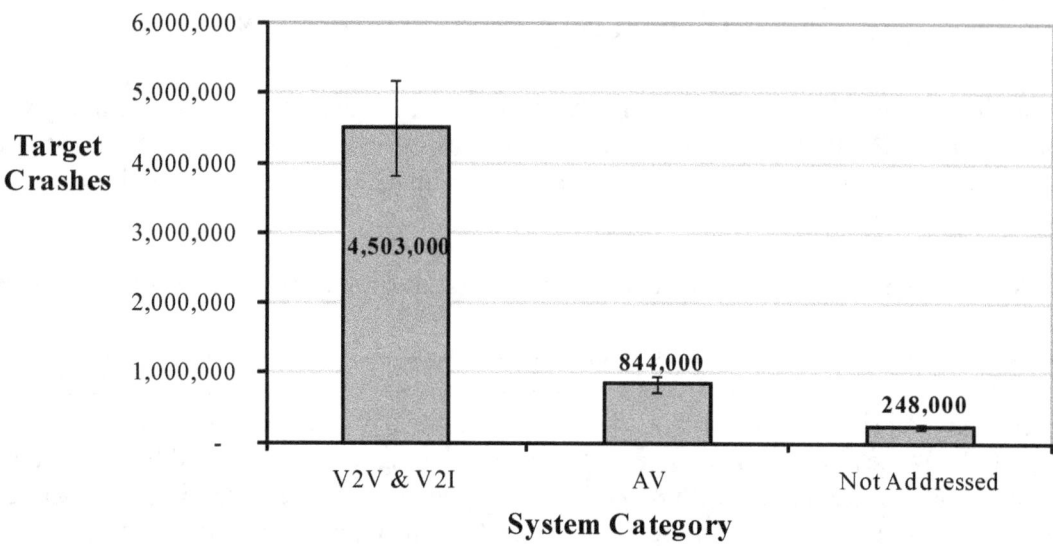

**Figure 16.** Annual Target All-Vehicle Crashes by System, Combined V2V and V2I Systems as Primary Countermeasure

### IV.2. Combined V2V and V2I Systems as Primary Countermeasure in Light-Vehicle Crashes

Combined V2V and V2I systems potentially address about 4,417,000 police-reported light-vehicle crashes annually, with the 95 percent confidence interval between 3,759,000 and 5,075,000. If considered as the primary countermeasure, these combined systems potentially address about 77 percent of all crashes involving at least one light vehicle. Excluding drivers impaired by alcohol or drowsiness, these systems deal with 83 percent of all light-vehicle crashes involving unimpaired drivers as shown in Figure 17. Figure 18 presents the annual target crash data and the 95 percent confidence intervals for each system category given combined V2V and V2I systems as the primary countermeasure. Table D2 in Appendix D lists the annual number of target light-vehicle crashes for each pre-crash scenario addressed by combined V2V and V2I systems as the primary countermeasure, as well as the annual number of remaining light-vehicle crashes tackled by AV systems.

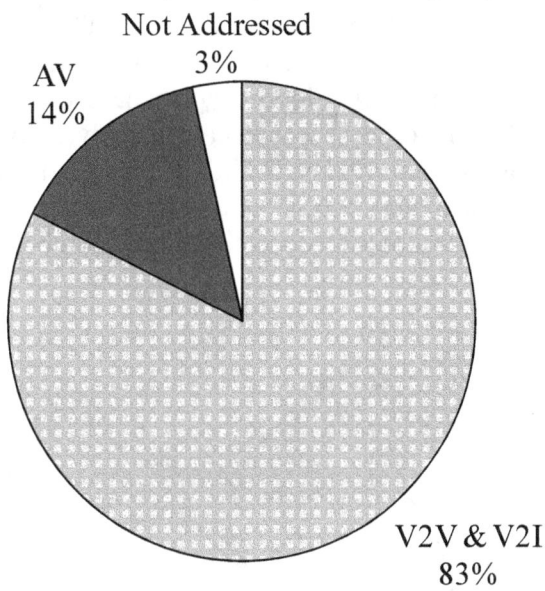

**Figure 17.** Distribution of Unimpaired Light-Vehicle Crashes by System, Combined V2V and V2I Systems as Primary Countermeasure

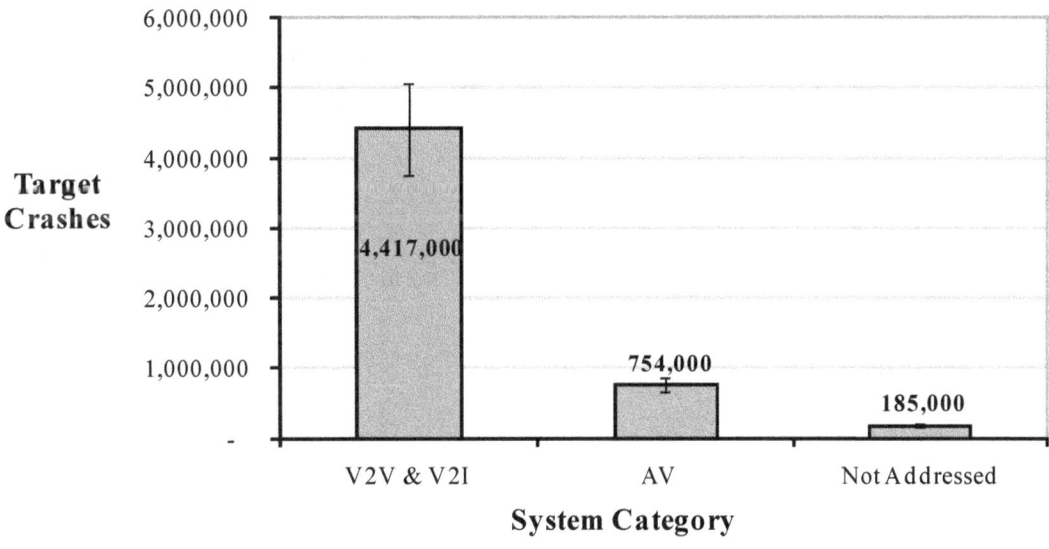

**Figure 18.** Annual Target Light-Vehicle Crashes by System, Combined V2V and V2I Systems as Primary Countermeasure

## IV.3. Combined V2V and V2I Systems as Primary Countermeasure in Heavy-Truck Crashes

Combined V2V and V2I systems potentially address about 272,000 police-reported heavy-truck crashes annually, with the 95 percent confidence interval between 233,000 and 311,000. If considered as the primary countermeasure, these combined systems potentially address about 71 percent of all crashes involving at least one heavy truck. Excluding drivers impaired by alcohol or drowsiness, these systems deal with 72 percent of all heavy-truck crashes involving unimpaired drivers as shown in Figure 19. Figure 20 presents the annual target crash data and the 95 percent confidence intervals for each system category given combined V2V and V2I systems as the primary countermeasure. Table D3 in Appendix D lists the annual number of target heavy-truck crashes for each pre-crash scenario addressed by combined V2V and V2I systems as the primary countermeasure, as well as the annual number of remaining heavy-truck crashes tackled by AV systems.

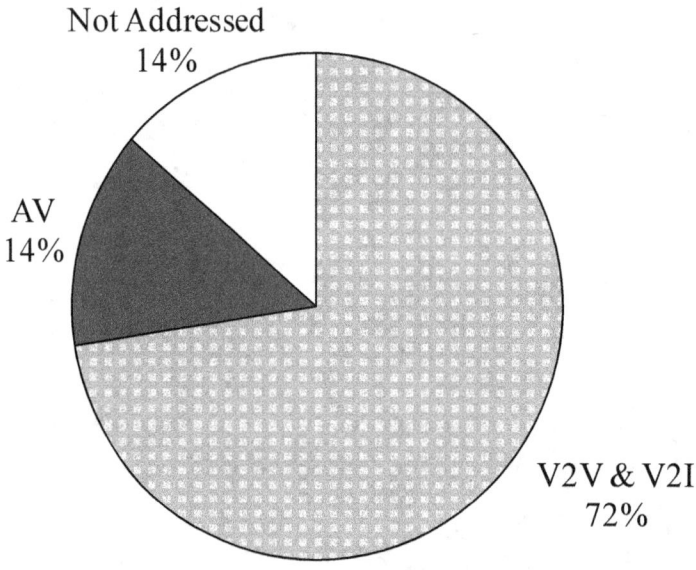

**Figure 19.** Distribution of Unimpaired Heavy-Truck Crashes by System, Combined V2V and V2I Systems as Primary Countermeasure

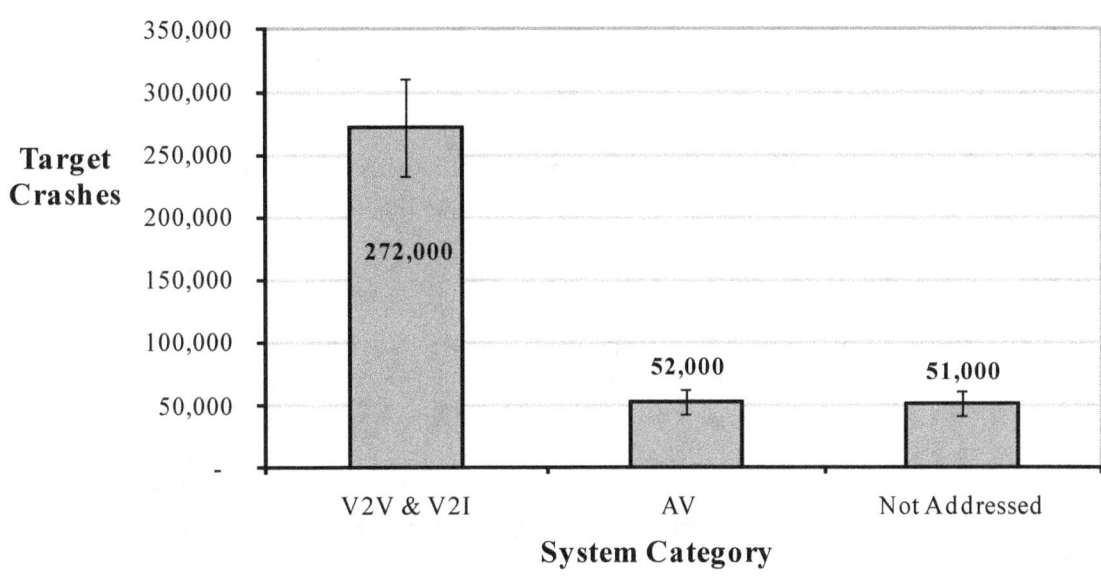

**Figure 20.** Annual Target Heavy-Truck Crashes by System, Combined V2V and V2I Systems as Primary Countermeasure

# V. CONCLUSIONS

## V.1. Analytical Results

The results of the analyses show the potential span of effectiveness for the various IntelliDrive categories of crash avoidance systems in each of the three crash types.

When analyzing the dataset of all police-reported crashes (5,977,000 annual average), the combined V2V and V2I systems potentially address approximately 4,503,000 or 75 percent. Figure 21 compares target crashes among the three system categories as well as the V2V and V2I combination. The error bars in Figure 21 refer to the 95 percent confidence intervals of the crash estimates. Figure 22 compares target crashes among the three system categories as proportions of all police-reported crashes involving all vehicle types. The proportion represents target crashes for each system category considered as a primary countermeasure. Table A4 in Appendix A shows the different criteria used to map applicable crash data to AV systems as the primary countermeasure and the remaining crashes to V2V and V2I systems.

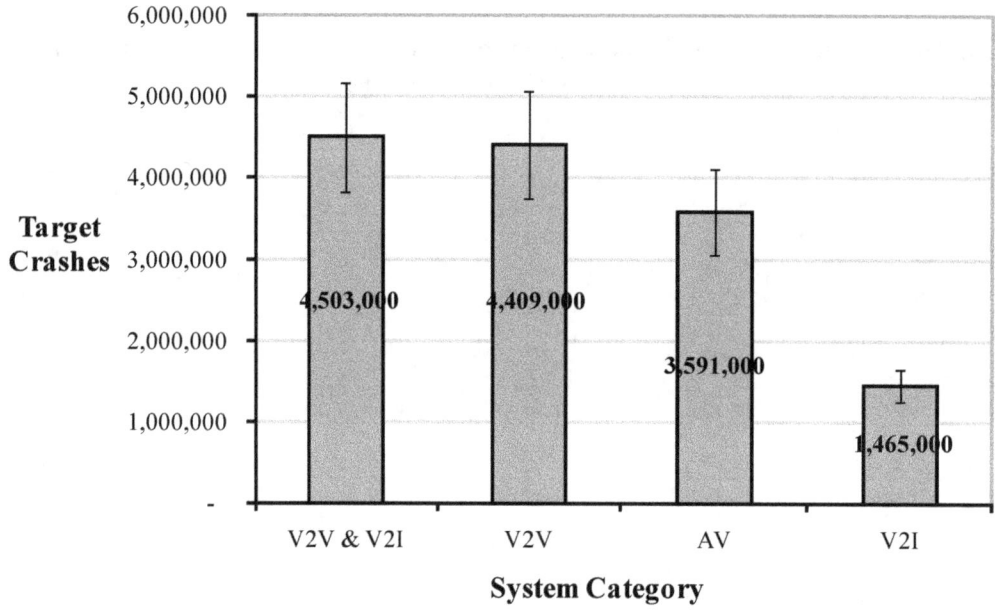

**Figure 21.** Comparison of Annual Target All-Vehicle Crashes Among System Categories

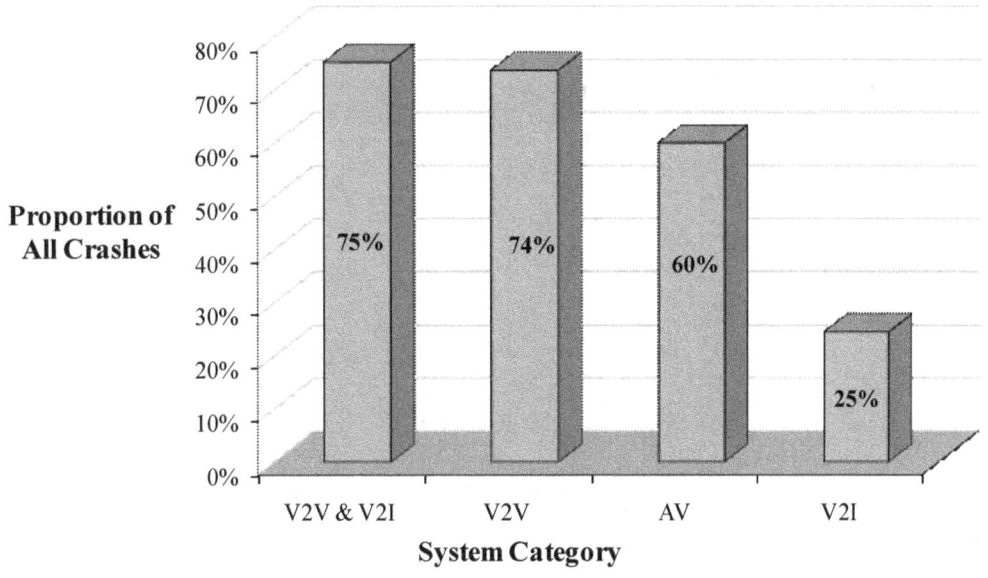

**Figure 22.** Comparison of Relative Target All-Vehicle Crashes
Among System Categories

When analyzing the dataset of all police-reported light-vehicle crashes (5,726,000 annual average), the combined V2V and V2I systems potentially address approximately 4,417,000 or 77 percent. Figure 23 compares target crashes among the three system categories as well as the V2V and V2I combination. The error bars in Figure 23 refer to the 95 percent confidence intervals of the crash estimates. Figure 24 compares target crashes among the three system categories as proportions of all police reported crashes involving light vehicle. The proportion represents target crashes for each system category considered as a primary countermeasure.

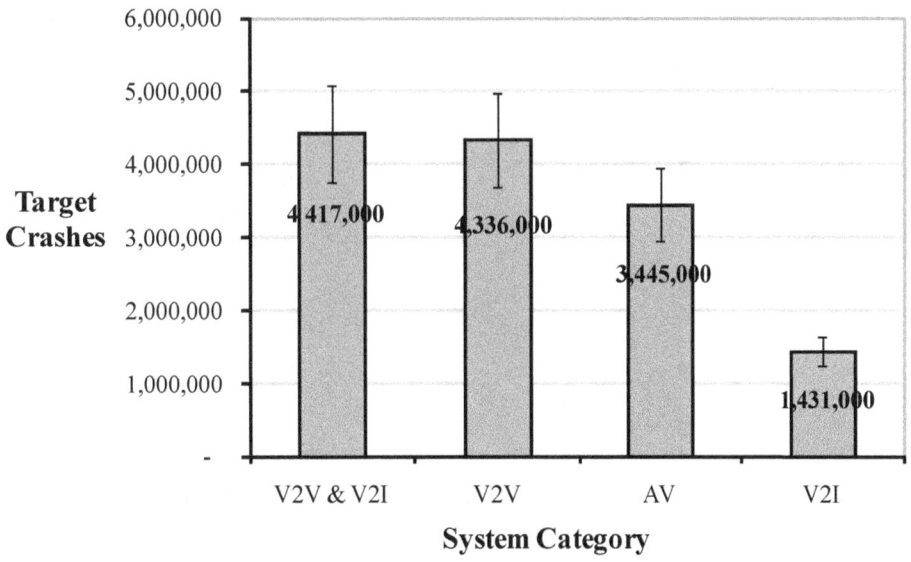

**Figure 23.** Comparison of Annual Target Light-Vehicle Crashes Among System Categories

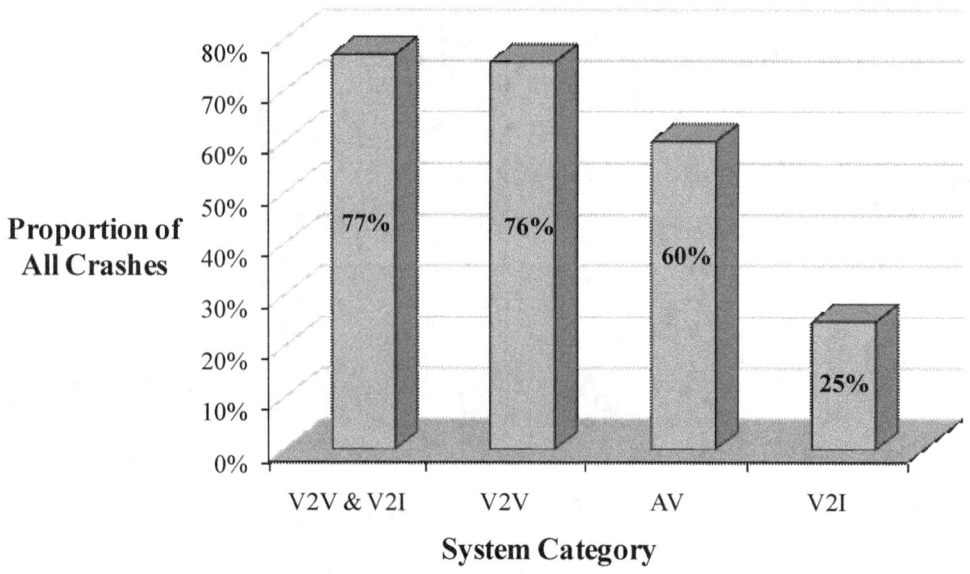

**Figure 24.** Comparison of Relative Target Light-Vehicle Crashes Among System Categories

When analyzing the dataset of all police-reported heavy-truck crashes (384,000 on average), the combined V2V and V2I systems potentially address approximately 272,000 or 71 percent. Figure 25 compares target crashes among the three system categories as well as the V2V and V2I combination. The error bars in Figure 25 refer to the 95 percent confidence intervals of the crash estimates. Figure 26 compares target crashes among the three system categories as proportions of all police-reported crashes involving at least one heavy truck. The proportion represents target crashes for each system category considered as a primary countermeasure.

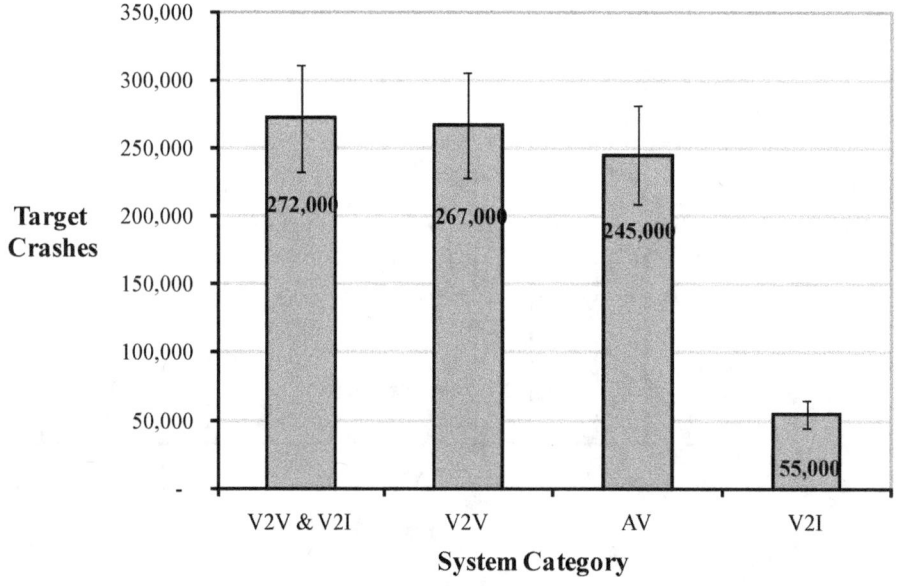

**Figure 25.** Comparison of Annual Target Heavy-Truck Crashes Among System Categories

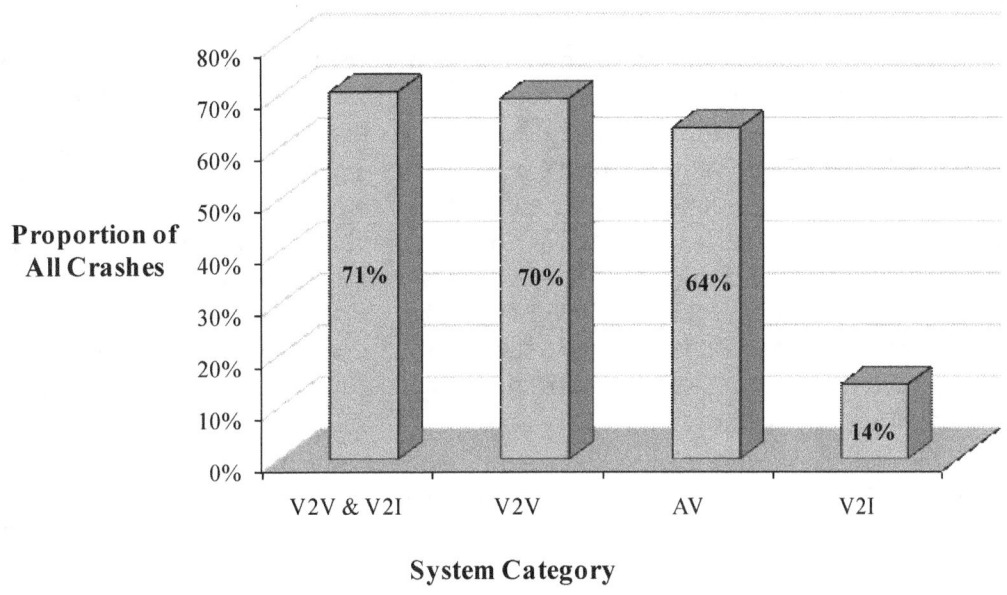

**Figure 26.** Comparison of Relative Target Heavy-Truck Crashes Among System Categories

Figure 27 summarizes the results of the percent applicability of V2V, V2I, and combined V2V and V2I systems to target all-vehicle, light-vehicle, and heavy-truck crashes. These systems potentially address a larger portion of light-vehicle crashes than all-vehicle and heavy-truck crashes. V2V systems have the potential to intervene in a more considerable number of crashes than V2I systems. Moreover, adding V2I to V2V systems appears to have an insignificant impact on raising the number of target crashes addressed by V2V systems alone.

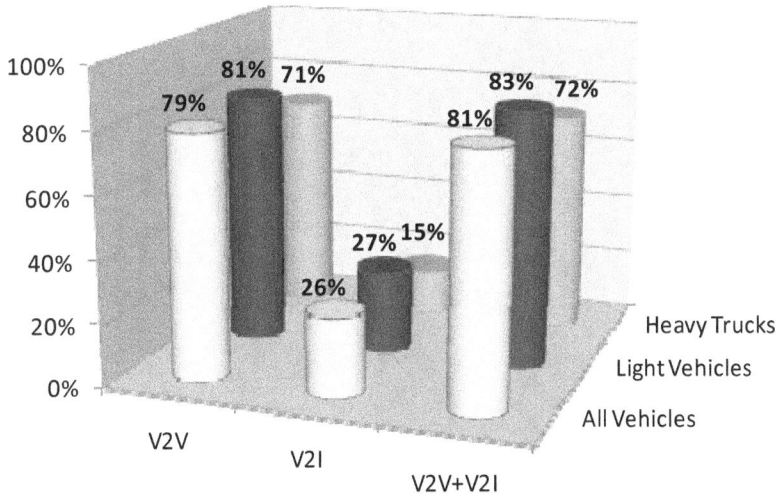

**Figure 27.** Percent Applicability of System Categories to Target Crash Types

## V.2. Follow-On Research

Follow-on research from this study will involve further updates from relevant databases to determine the societal costs, describe crash circumstances, identify crash contributing and causal factors, and quantify the kinematics of pre-crash scenarios. In addition to the NASS GES crash databases, the National Motor Vehicle Crash Causation Survey database provides information about the circumstances, contributing factors, and causes of crashes involving light vehicles. Event Data Recorder data from cases in the NASS Crashworthiness Data System may also be incorporated to quantify the kinematics of light vehicles in terms of travel speed, brake application, and deceleration level applied over a span of five seconds before the crash. The Large Truck Crash Causation Study as well as the NASS GES crash databases contain the information needed to statistically describe the circumstances, contributing factors, and causes of pre-crash scenarios involving heavy trucks.

Updating the statistical description of pre-crash scenarios will serve to rank pre-crash scenarios according to frequency and severity, crash type, and pre-crash characteristics. Ranking will be based not only on the frequency of occurrence, but also on the crash severity measured by comprehensive economic costs (values of statistical life) and functional years lost. Moreover, data on frequency and severity ranking, crash type, and pre-crash characteristics will be analyzed to identify logical groupings of pre-crash scenarios that might potentially be addressed by a selected set of IntelliDrive safety applications.

This report focused on safety applications in support of the IntelliDrive safety initiative, which involve communications among vehicles (V2V) and between vehicles and the infrastructure (V2I). Thus, results were presented for potential V2V, V2I, and V2V/V2I safety applications. The results of autonomous vehicle (AV) safety systems were provided for comparison purposes. Separate analyses are recommended to examine the incremental target crash population that might be potentially addressed by the V2V/AV, V2I/AV, and V2V/V2I/AV combinations.

## VI. REFERENCES

[1] USDOT IntelliDrive Program: Vehicle to Vehicle Safety Application Research Plan. (2010, January 10). PowerPoint presentation. Washington, DC: National Highway Traffic Safety Administration and Research and Innovative Technology Administration. Available at http://www.fmcsa.dot.gov/facts-research/media/webinar-10-01-20-slides.pdf.

[2] ITS Strategic Research Plan, 2010-2014: Transforming Transportation Through Connectivity. (2009, December 8). PowerPoint presentation FHWA-JPO-10-028. Washington, DC: ITS Joint Program Office, Research and Innovative Technology Administration.  Available at http://www.its.dot.gov/strat_plan/index.htm.

[3] National Automotive Sampling System (NASS) General Estimates System (GES) - Analytical User's Manual 1988-2008. (2009). Washington, DC: National Center for Statistics and Analysis, National Highway Traffic Safety Administration. Available at http://www-nrd.nhtsa.dot.gov/Pubs/AUM08.PDF.

[4] Najm, W. G., Smith, J. D., & Yanagisawa, M. (2007, April). Pre-Crash Scenario Typology for Crash Avoidance Research.  DOT HS 810 767. Washington, DC: National Highway Traffic Safety Administration.

[5] CAMP. (2006, April). Vehicle Safety Communications Project - Final Report.  DOT HS 810 591. Washington, DC:  National Highway Traffic Safety Administration.

[6] Ahmed-Zaid, F., & Carter, A. (2009, January). Vehicle Safety Communications – Applications First Annual Report.  DOT HS 811 073. Washington, DC: National Highway Traffic Safety Administration. Available at http://www.safercar.gov/staticfiles/DOT/NHTSA/NRD/Multimedia/PDFs/Crash%20Avoidan ce/2009/811073.pdf.

[7] Cooperative Intersection Collision Avoidance Systems. Washington, DC: ITS Joint Program Office, Research and Innovative Technology Administration. Available at http://www.its.dot.gov/cicas/

## Appendix A. Mapping of Pre-Crash Scenarios to System Categories

**Table A1.** Mapping of Pre-Crash Scenarios to System Categories - V2V System Primary

| Pre-Crash Scenario | V2V | V2I | AV |
|---|---|---|---|
| No driver present | None | None | None |
| Vehicle failure | None | None | All Crashes |
| Control loss/vehicle action | All Crashes | None Remaining | None Remaining |
| Control loss/no vehicle action | All Crashes | None Remaining | None Remaining |
| Running red light | 2+ Vehicle Crashes | All Remaining Crashes | None Remaining |
| Running stop sign | 2+ Vehicle Crashes | All Remaining Crashes | All Remaining Crashes |
| Road edge departure/maneuver | None | Speeding Crashes | Conditional Speeding Crashes |
| Road edge departure/no maneuver | None | Speeding Crashes | All Crashes |
| Road edge departure/backing | None | None | All Crashes |
| Animal/maneuver | None | None | All Crashes |
| Animal/no maneuver | None | None | All Crashes |
| Pedestrian/maneuver | None | Crosswalk Crashes | All Crashes |
| Pedestrian/no maneuver | None | Crosswalk Crashes | All Crashes |
| Cyclist/maneuver | None | None | All Crashes |
| Cyclist/no maneuver | None | None | All Crashes |
| Backing into vehicle | All Crashes | None | None |
| Turning/same direction | All Crashes | None | None Remaining |
| Parking/same direction | All Crashes | None | None Remaining |
| Changing lanes/same direction | All Crashes | None | None Remaining |
| Drifting/same lane | All Crashes | None | None Remaining |
| Opposite direction/maneuver | All Crashes | None | None Remaining |
| Opposite direction/no maneuver | All Crashes | None | None Remaining |
| Rear-end/striking maneuver | All Crashes | None | None Remaining |
| Rear-end/lead vehicle accelerating | All Crashes | None | None Remaining |
| Rear-end/lead vehicle constant speed | All Crashes | None | None Remaining |
| Rear-end/lead vehicle decelerating | All Crashes | None | None Remaining |
| Rear-end/lead vehicle stopped | All Crashes | None | None Remaining |
| LTAP/OD @ signal | All Crashes | None Remaining | None |
| Turn right @ signal | All Crashes | None Remaining | None |
| LTAP/OD @ non signal | All Crashes | None Remaining | None |
| SCP @ non signal | All Crashes | None Remaining | None |
| Turn @ non signal | All Crashes | None Remaining | None |
| Evasive maneuver/maneuver | Uncertain | Uncertain | Uncertain |
| Evasive maneuver/no maneuver | Uncertain | Uncertain | Uncertain |
| Rollover | None | Speeding Crashes | Conditional Speeding Crashes |
| Noncollision - No impact | None | None | None |
| Object contacted/maneuver | None | Speeding Crashes | Conditional Speeding Crashes |
| Object contacted/no maneuver | None | Speeding Crashes | All Crashes |
| Hit and run | Uncertain | Uncertain | Uncertain |
| Other - Rear-end | All Crashes | None | None Remaining |
| Other - Sideswipe | All Crashes | None | None Remaining |
| Other - Turn Across Path | All Crashes | None Remaining | None |
| Other - Turn Into Path | All Crashes | None Remaining | None |
| Other | Uncertain | Uncertain | Uncertain |

| | |
|---|---|
| 2+ Vehicle Crashes | Countermeasure addresses crashes involving at least 2 vehicles in transport |
| All Crashes | Countermeasure addresses all crashes |
| All Remaining Crashes | Countermeasure addresses all remaining crashes not addressed by primary countermeasure |
| Conditional Speeding Crashes | Countermeasure addresses all speeding crashes except those occurring on slippery surface in clear weather |
| Crosswalk Crashes | Countermeasure addresses all pedestrian crashes occurring in crosswalks |
| None | Countermeasure does not address any crashes |
| None Remaining | Primary countermeasure addresses all crashes |
| Speeding Crashes | Countermeasure addresses all crashes cited with speeding |
| Uncertain | Insufficient crash information to assess countermeasure applicability |
| Intersection crashes | Countermeasure addresses all crashes occurring at intersections only |

| | |
|---|---|
| LTAP/OD | Left Turn Across Path/Opposite Directions |
| SCP | Straight Crossing Paths |

It is generally assumed that V2V safety applications would potentially address all crashes that involve at least two vehicles equipped with basic V2V equipment. It is noteworthy that "not addressed" crashes include "uncertain" and "none" crashes in the table above.

**Table A2.** Mapping of Pre-Crash Scenarios to System Categories - V2I System Primary

| Pre-Crash Scenario | V2I | V2V | AV |
|---|---|---|---|
| No driver present | None | None | None |
| Vehicle failure | None | None | All Crashes |
| Control loss/vehicle action | Speeding Crashes | All Remaining Crashes | None Remaining |
| Control loss/no vehicle action | Speeding Crashes | All Remaining Crashes | None Remaining |
| Running red light | All Crashes | None Remaining | None Remaining |
| Running stop sign | All Crashes | None Remaining | None Remaining |
| Road edge departure/maneuver | Speeding Crashes | None | None Remaining |
| Road edge departure/no maneuver | Speeding Crashes | None | All Remaining Crashes |
| Road edge departure/backing | None | None | All Crashes |
| Animal/maneuver | None | None | All Crashes |
| Animal/no maneuver | None | None | All Crashes |
| Pedestrian/maneuver | Crosswalk Crashes | None | All Remaining Crashes |
| Pedestrian/no maneuver | Crosswalk Crashes | None | All Remaining Crashes |
| Cyclist/maneuver | None | None | All Crashes |
| Cyclist/no maneuver | None | None | All Crashes |
| Backing into vehicle | None | All Crashes | None |
| Turning/same direction | None | All Crashes | All Crashes |
| Parking/same direction | None | All Crashes | All Crashes |
| Changing lanes/same direction | None | All Crashes | All Crashes |
| Drifting/same lane | None | All Crashes | All Crashes |
| Opposite direction/maneuver | None | All Crashes | None |
| Opposite direction/no maneuver | None | All Crashes | All Crashes |
| Rear-end/striking maneuver | None | All Crashes | All Crashes |
| Rear-end/lead vehicle accelerating | None | All Crashes | All Crashes |
| Rear-end/lead vehicle constant speed | None | All Crashes | All Crashes |
| Rear-end/lead vehicle decelerating | None | All Crashes | All Crashes |
| Rear-end/Lead vehicle stopped | None | All Crashes | All Crashes |
| LTAP/OD @ signal | All Crashes | None Remaining | None |
| Turn right @ signal | All Crashes | None Remaining | None |
| LTAP/OD @ non signal | Intersection Crashes | All Remaining Crashes | None |
| SCP @ non signal | Intersection Crashes | All Remaining Crashes | None |
| Turn @ non signal | Intersection Crashes | All Remaining Crashes | None |
| Evasive maneuver/maneuver | Uncertain | Uncertain | Uncertain |
| Evasive maneuver/no maneuver | Uncertain | Uncertain | Uncertain |
| Rollover | Speeding Crashes | None | None Remaining |
| Noncollision - No impact | None | None | None |
| Object contacted/maneuver | Speeding Crashes | None | None Remaining |
| Object contacted/no maneuver | Speeding Crashes | None | All Remaining Crashes |
| Hit and run | Uncertain | Uncertain | Uncertain |
| Other - Rear-end | None | All Crashes | All Crashes |
| Other - Sideswipe | None | All Crashes | All Crashes |
| Other - Turn Across Path | Intersection Crashes | All Remaining Crashes | None |
| Other - Turn Into Path | Intersection Crashes | All Remaining Crashes | None |
| Other | Uncertain | Uncertain | Uncertain |

| Control loss | Excessive speed warning that alerts vehicles of overspeeding for the prevailing conditions. |
|---|---|
| Running red light | Red light violation warning system |
| Running stop sign | Stop sign violation warning system |
| Road edge departure | Excessive speed warning that alerts vehicles of overspeeding for the prevailing conditions. |
| Pedestrian | Pedestrian crossing information at designated intersections |
| LTAP/OD & Turn right @ signal | Intersection collision warning |
| LTAP/OD, SCP, & Turn @ non signal | Intersection collision warning only at intersections, excluding driveways & other locations. |
| Rollover | Excessive speed warning that alerts vehicles of overspeeding for the prevailing conditions. |
| Object contacted | Excessive speed warning that alerts vehicles of overspeeding for the prevailing conditions. |

**Table A3.** Mapping of Pre-Crash Scenarios to System Categories – V2V+V2I System Primary

| Pre-Crash Scenario | V2V & V2I | AV |
|---|---|---|
| No driver present | None | None |
| Vehicle failure | None | All Crashes |
| Control loss/vehicle action | All Crashes | None Remaining |
| Control loss/no vehicle action | All Crashes | None Remaining |
| Running red light | All Crashes | None Remaining |
| Running stop sign | All Crashes | None Remaining |
| Road edge departure/maneuver | Speeding Crashes | None Remaining |
| Road edge departure/no maneuver | Speeding Crashes | All Remaining Crashes |
| Road edge departure/backing | None | All Crashes |
| Animal/maneuver | None | All Crashes |
| Animal/no maneuver | None | All Crashes |
| Pedestrian/maneuver | Crosswalk Crashes | All Remaining Crashes |
| Pedestrian/no maneuver | Crosswalk Crashes | All Remaining Crashes |
| Cyclist/maneuver | None | All Crashes |
| Cyclist/no maneuver | None | All Crashes |
| Backing into vehicle | All Crashes | None |
| Turning/same direction | All Crashes | None Remaining |
| Parking/same direction | All Crashes | None Remaining |
| Changing lanes/same direction | All Crashes | None Remaining |
| Drifting/same lane | All Crashes | None Remaining |
| Opposite direction/maneuver | All Crashes | None Remaining |
| Opposite direction/no maneuver | All Crashes | None Remaining |
| Rear-end/striking maneuver | All Crashes | None Remaining |
| Rear-end/lead vehicle accelerating | All Crashes | None Remaining |
| Rear-end/lead vehicle constant speed | All Crashes | None Remaining |
| Rear-end/lead vehicle decelerating | All Crashes | None Remaining |
| Rear-end/lead vehicle stopped | All Crashes | None Remaining |
| LTAP/OD @ signal | All Crashes | None |
| Turn right @ signal | All Crashes | None |
| LTAP/OD @ non signal | All Crashes | None |
| SCP @ non signal | All Crashes | None |
| Turn @ non signal | All Crashes | None |
| Evasive maneuver/maneuver | Uncertain | Uncertain |
| Evasive maneuver/no maneuver | Uncertain | Uncertain |
| Rollover | Speeding Crashes | None Remaining |
| Noncollision - No impact | None | None |
| Object contacted/maneuver | Speeding Crashes | None Remaining |
| Object contacted/no maneuver | Speeding Crashes | All Remaining Crashes |
| Hit and run | Uncertain | Uncertain |
| Other - Rear-end | All Crashes | None Remaining |
| Other - Sideswipe | All Crashes | None Remaining |
| Other - Turn Across Path | All Crashes | None |
| Other - Turn Into Path | All Crashes | None |
| Other | Uncertain | Uncertain |

**Table A4.** Mapping of Pre-Crash Scenarios to System Categories – AV System Primary

| Pre-Crash Scenario | AV | V2V | V2I |
|---|---|---|---|
| No driver present | None | None | None |
| Vehicle failure | All Crashes | None | None |
| Control loss/vehicle action | Conditional Speeding Crashes | All Remaining Crashes | All Remaining Speeding Crashes |
| Control loss/no vehicle action | Conditional Speeding Crashes | All Remaining Crashes | All Remaining Speeding Crashes |
| Running red light | Single-Vehicle Crashes | All Remaining Crashes | All Remaining Crashes |
| Running stop sign | All Crashes | None Remaining | None Remaining |
| Road edge departure/maneuver | Conditional Speeding Crashes | None | All Remaining Speeding Crashes |
| Road edge departure/no maneuver | All Crashes | None | None Remaining |
| Road edge departure/backing | All Crashes | None | None |
| Animal/maneuver | All Crashes | None | None |
| Animal/no maneuver | All Crashes | None | None |
| Pedestrian/maneuver | All Crashes | None | None Remaining |
| Pedestrian/no maneuver | All Crashes | None | None Remaining |
| Cyclist/maneuver | All Crashes | None | None |
| Cyclist/no maneuver | All Crashes | None | None |
| Backing into vehicle | None | All Crashes | None |
| Turning/same direction | All Crashes | None Remaining | None |
| Parking/same direction | All Crashes | None Remaining | None |
| Changing lanes/same direction | All Crashes | None Remaining | None |
| Drifting/same lane | All Crashes | None Remaining | None |
| Opposite direction/maneuver | None | All Crashes | None |
| Opposite direction/no maneuver | All Crashes | None Remaining | None |
| Rear-end/striking maneuver | All Crashes | None Remaining | None |
| Rear-end/lead vehicle accelerating | All Crashes | None Remaining | None |
| Rear-end/lead vehicle constant speed | All Crashes | None Remaining | None |
| Rear-end/lead vehicle decelerating | All Crashes | None Remaining | None |
| Rear-end/Lead vehicle stopped | All Crashes | None Remaining | None |
| LTAP/OD @ signal | None | All Crashes | All Crashes |
| Turn right @ signal | None | All Crashes | All Crashes |
| LTAP/OD @ non signal | None | All Crashes | Intersection Crashes |
| SCP @ non signal | None | All Crashes | Intersection Crashes |
| Turn @ non signal | None | All Crashes | Intersection Crashes |
| Evasive maneuver/maneuver | Uncertain | Uncertain | Uncertain |
| Evasive maneuver/no maneuver | Uncertain | Uncertain | Uncertain |
| Rollover | Conditional Speeding Crashes | None | All Remaining Speeding Crashes |
| Noncollision - No impact | None | None | None |
| Object contacted/maneuver | Conditional Speeding Crashes | None | All Remaining Speeding Crashes |
| Object contacted/no maneuver | All Crashes | None | None Remaining |
| Hit and run | Uncertain | Uncertain | Uncertain |
| Other - Rear-end | All Crashes | None Remaining | None |
| Other - Sideswipe | All Crashes | None Remaining | None |
| Other - Turn Across Path | None | All Crashes | Intersection Crashes |
| Other - Turn Into Path | None | All Crashes | Intersection Crashes |
| Other | Uncertain | Uncertain | Uncertain |

| | |
|---|---|
| Vehicle failure | Component status monitor that alerts the driver to a potential failure in tire, brake, engine, etc. |
| Control loss | Excessive speed warning that correlates map information to vehicle speed and controls. |
| Running red light | Lane departure warning, lane keeping system, or obstacle detection warning |
| Running stop sign | Stop sign violation warning that correlates map information to vehicle speed and controls. |
| Road edge departure | Lane departure warning or lane keeping system in pre-event no maneuver. |
| Road edge departure/backing | Back up warning system that detects objects and parked vehicles directly behind vehicle. |
| Animal/pedestrian/cyclist | Forward crash warning that detects animals, pedestrians, or cyclists. |
| Backing into vehicle | None since this involves vehicles in pre-event perpendicular directions where host is backing & turning. |
| Turning/parking/changing lanes/drifting | Lane change warning or blind spot detection |
| Opposite direction | Lane departure warning or lane keeping system in pre-event no maneuver. |
| Rear-end scenarios | Rear-end crash warning or adaptive cruise control. |
| Rollover | Excessive speed warning that correlates map information to vehicle speed and controls. |
| Object contacted/maneuver | Excessive speed warning that correlates map information to vehicle speed and controls. |
| Object contacted/no maneuver | Lane departure warning or lane keeping system in pre-event no maneuver. |

# Appendix B. Distribution of Pre-Crash Scenario by System Category–V2V System Primary

**Table B1.** Target All-Vehicle Crash Data for V2V Systems as Primary Countermeasure

| Pre-Crash Scenario | All Crashes | V2V | AV | V2I |
|---|---|---|---|---|
| No driver present | 1,000 | - | - | - |
| Vehicle failure | 50,000 | - | 50,000 | - |
| Control loss/vehicle action | 97,000 | 97,000 | - | - |
| Control loss/no vehicle action | 442,000 | 442,000 | - | - |
| Running red light | 226,000 | 226,000 | - | 1,000 |
| Running stop sign | 42,000 | 39,000 | 3,000 | 3,000 |
| Road edge departure/maneuver | 74,000 | - | 9,000 | 10,000 |
| Road edge departure/no maneuver | 277,000 | - | 277,000 | 54,000 |
| Road edge departure/backing | 82,000 | - | 82,000 | - |
| Animal/maneuver | 18,000 | - | 18,000 | - |
| Animal/no maneuver | 296,000 | - | 296,000 | - |
| Pedestrian/maneuver | 21,000 | - | 21,000 | 8,000 |
| Pedestrian/no maneuver | 42,000 | - | 42,000 | 5,000 |
| Cyclist/maneuver | 21,000 | - | 21,000 | - |
| Cyclist/no maneuver | 29,000 | - | 29,000 | - |
| Backing into vehicle | 129,000 | 129,000 | - | - |
| Turning/same direction | 197,000 | 197,000 | - | - |
| Parking/same direction | 38,000 | 38,000 | - | - |
| Changing lanes/same direction | 334,000 | 334,000 | - | - |
| Drifting/same lane | 105,000 | 105,000 | - | - |
| Opposite direction/maneuver | 9,000 | 9,000 | - | - |
| Opposite direction/no maneuver | 108,000 | 108,000 | - | - |
| Rear-end/striking maneuver | 81,000 | 81,000 | - | - |
| Rear-end/LVA | 22,000 | 22,000 | - | - |
| Rear-end/LVM | 192,000 | 192,000 | - | - |
| Rear-end/LVD | 388,000 | 388,000 | - | - |
| Rear-end/LVS | 910,000 | 910,000 | - | - |
| LTAP/OD @ signal | 195,000 | 195,000 | - | - |
| Turn right @ signal | 30,000 | 30,000 | - | - |
| LTAP/OD @ non signal | 179,000 | 179,000 | - | - |
| SCP @ non signal | 637,000 | 637,000 | - | - |
| Turn @ non signal | 45,000 | 45,000 | - | - |
| Evasive maneuver/maneuver | 12,000 | - | - | - |
| Evasive maneuver/no maneuver | 45,000 | - | - | - |
| Rollover | 6,000 | - | 1,000 | 1,000 |
| Noncollision - No impact | 36,000 | - | - | - |
| Object contacted/maneuver | 66,000 | - | 4,000 | 5,000 |
| Object contacted/no maneuver | 82,000 | - | 82,000 | 7,000 |
| Hit and run | 3,000 | - | - | - |
| Other - Rear-end | 1,000 | 1,000 | - | - |
| Other - Sideswipe | 2,000 | 2,000 | - | - |
| Other - Turn Across Path | 1,000 | 1,000 | - | - |
| Other - Turn Into Path | 1,000 | 1,000 | - | - |
| Other | 22,000 | - | - | - |
|  | 5,595,000 | 4,409,000 | 935,000 | 94,000 |

**Table B2.** Target Light-Vehicle Crash Data for V2V Systems as Primary Countermeasure

| Pre-Crash Scenario | All Crashes | V2V | AV | V2I |
|---|---|---|---|---|
| No driver present | 1,000 | - | - | - |
| Vehicle failure | 45,000 | - | 45,000 | - |
| Control loss/vehicle action | 89,000 | 89,000 | - | - |
| Control loss/no vehicle action | 414,000 | 414,000 | - | - |
| Running red light | 226,000 | 225,000 | - | 1,000 |
| Running stop sign | 42,000 | 39,000 | 2,000 | 2,000 |
| Road edge departure/maneuver | 54,000 | - | 8,000 | 9,000 |
| Road edge departure/no maneuver | 240,000 | - | 240,000 | 48,000 |
| Road edge departure/backing | 68,000 | - | 68,000 | - |
| Animal/maneuver | 15,000 | - | 15,000 | - |
| Animal/no maneuver | 285,000 | - | 285,000 | - |
| Pedestrian/maneuver | 19,000 | - | 19,000 | 8,000 |
| Pedestrian/no maneuver | 39,000 | - | 39,000 | 5,000 |
| Cyclist/maneuver | 20,000 | - | 20,000 | - |
| Cyclist/no maneuver | 27,000 | - | 27,000 | - |
| Backing into vehicle | 127,000 | 127,000 | - | - |
| Turning/same direction | 195,000 | 195,000 | - | - |
| Parking/same direction | 38,000 | 38,000 | - | - |
| Changing lanes/same direction | 329,000 | 329,000 | - | - |
| Drifting/same lane | 102,000 | 102,000 | - | - |
| Opposite direction/maneuver | 9,000 | 9,000 | - | - |
| Opposite direction/no maneuver | 102,000 | 102,000 | - | - |
| Rear-end/striking maneuver | 80,000 | 80,000 | - | - |
| Rear-end/LVA | 22,000 | 22,000 | - | - |
| Rear-end/LVM | 190,000 | 190,000 | - | - |
| Rear-end/LVD | 384,000 | 384,000 | - | - |
| Rear-end/LVS | 906,000 | 906,000 | - | - |
| LTAP/OD @ signal | 195,000 | 195,000 | - | - |
| Turn right @ signal | 29,000 | 29,000 | - | - |
| LTAP/OD @ non signal | 178,000 | 178,000 | - | - |
| SCP @ non signal | 634,000 | 634,000 | - | - |
| Turn @ non signal | 43,000 | 43,000 | - | - |
| Evasive maneuver/maneuver | 12,000 | - | - | - |
| Evasive maneuver/no maneuver | 43,000 | - | - | - |
| Rollover | 3,000 | - | 1,000 | 1,000 |
| Noncollision - No impact | 30,000 | - | - | - |
| Object contacted/maneuver | 32,000 | - | 2,000 | 3,000 |
| Object contacted/no maneuver | 61,000 | - | 61,000 | 5,000 |
| Hit and run | 3,000 | - | - | - |
| Other - Rear-end | 1,000 | 1,000 | - | - |
| Other - Sideswipe | 2,000 | 2,000 | - | - |
| Other - Turn Across Path | 1,000 | 1,000 | - | - |
| Other - Turn Into Path | 1,000 | 1,000 | - | - |
| Other | 21,000 | - | - | - |
| | 5,356,000 | 4,336,000 | 833,000 | 81,000 |

**Table B3.** Target Heavy-Truck Crash Data for V2V Systems as Primary Countermeasure

| Pre-Crash Scenario | All Crashes | V2V | AV | V2I |
|---|---|---|---|---|
| No driver present | - | - | - | - |
| Vehicle failure | 5,000 | - | 5,000 | - |
| Control loss/vehicle action | 5,000 | 5,000 | - | - |
| Control loss/no vehicle action | 16,000 | 16,000 | - | - |
| Running red light | 9,000 | 9,000 | - | - |
| Running stop sign | 2,000 | 1,000 | - | - |
| Road edge departure/maneuver | 14,000 | - | 1,000 | 1,000 |
| Road edge departure/no maneuver | 17,000 | - | 17,000 | 2,000 |
| Road edge departure/backing | 8,000 | - | 8,000 | - |
| Animal/maneuver | 2,000 | - | 2,000 | - |
| Animal/no maneuver | 5,000 | - | 5,000 | - |
| Pedestrian/maneuver | 1,000 | - | 1,000 | - |
| Pedestrian/no maneuver | 1,000 | - | 1,000 | - |
| Cyclist/maneuver | - | - | - | - |
| Cyclist/no maneuver | - | - | - | - |
| Backing into vehicle | 19,000 | 19,000 | - | - |
| Turning/same direction | 28,000 | 28,000 | - | - |
| Parking/same direction | 3,000 | 3,000 | - | - |
| Changing lanes/same direction | 49,000 | 49,000 | - | - |
| Drifting/same lane | 20,000 | 20,000 | - | - |
| Opposite direction/maneuver | 1,000 | 1,000 | - | - |
| Opposite direction/no maneuver | 13,000 | 13,000 | - | - |
| Rear-end/striking maneuver | 4,000 | 4,000 | - | - |
| Rear-end/LVA | 1,000 | 1,000 | - | - |
| Rear-end/LVM | 13,000 | 13,000 | - | - |
| Rear-end/LVD | 17,000 | 17,000 | - | - |
| Rear-end/LVS | 29,000 | 29,000 | - | - |
| LTAP/OD @ signal | 5,000 | 5,000 | - | - |
| Turn right @ signal | 3,000 | 3,000 | - | - |
| LTAP/OD @ non signal | 5,000 | 5,000 | - | - |
| SCP @ non signal | 22,000 | 22,000 | - | - |
| Turn @ non signal | 5,000 | 5,000 | - | - |
| Evasive maneuver/maneuver | 1,000 | - | - | - |
| Evasive maneuver/no maneuver | 3,000 | - | - | - |
| Rollover | 1,000 | - | - | - |
| Noncollision - No impact | 11,000 | - | - | - |
| Object contacted/maneuver | 19,000 | - | - | 1,000 |
| Object contacted/no maneuver | 17,000 | - | 17,000 | 1,000 |
| Hit and run | 1,000 | - | - | - |
| Other - Rear-end | - | - | - | - |
| Other - Sideswipe | - | - | - | - |
| Other - Turn Across Path | - | - | - | - |
| Other - Turn Into Path | - | - | - | - |
| Other | 3,000 | - | - | - |
|  | 375,000 | 267,000 | 57,000 | 5,000 |

35

## Appendix C. Distribution of Pre-Crash Scenario by System Category–V2I System Primary
**Table C1.** Target All-Vehicle Crash Data for V2I Systems as Primary Countermeasure

| Pre-Crash Scenario | All Crashes | V2I | AV | V2V |
|---|---|---|---|---|
| No driver present | 1,000 | - | - | - |
| Vehicle failure | 50,000 | - | 50,000 | - |
| Control loss/vehicle action | 97,000 | 59,000 | - | 38,000 |
| Control loss/no vehicle action | 442,000 | 252,000 | - | 190,000 |
| Running red light | 226,000 | 226,000 | - | - |
| Running stop sign | 42,000 | 42,000 | - | - |
| Road edge departure/maneuver | 74,000 | 10,000 | - | - |
| Road edge departure/no maneuver | 277,000 | 54,000 | 223,000 | - |
| Road edge departure/backing | 82,000 | - | 82,000 | - |
| Animal/maneuver | 18,000 | - | 18,000 | - |
| Animal/no maneuver | 296,000 | - | 296,000 | - |
| Pedestrian/maneuver | 21,000 | 8,000 | 13,000 | - |
| Pedestrian/no maneuver | 42,000 | 5,000 | 37,000 | - |
| Cyclist/maneuver | 21,000 | - | 21,000 | - |
| Cyclist/no maneuver | 29,000 | - | 29,000 | - |
| Backing into vehicle | 129,000 | - | - | 129,000 |
| Turning/same direction | 197,000 | - | 197,000 | 197,000 |
| Parking/same direction | 38,000 | - | 38,000 | 38,000 |
| Changing lanes/same direction | 334,000 | - | 334,000 | 334,000 |
| Drifting/same lane | 105,000 | - | 105,000 | 105,000 |
| Opposite direction/maneuver | 9,000 | - | - | 9,000 |
| Opposite direction/no maneuver | 108,000 | - | 108,000 | 108,000 |
| Rear-end/striking maneuver | 81,000 | - | 81,000 | 81,000 |
| Rear-end/LVA | 22,000 | - | 22,000 | 22,000 |
| Rear-end/LVM | 192,000 | - | 192,000 | 192,000 |
| Rear-end/LVD | 388,000 | - | 388,000 | 388,000 |
| Rear-end/LVS | 910,000 | - | 910,000 | 910,000 |
| LTAP/OD @ signal | 195,000 | 195,000 | - | - |
| Turn right @ signal | 30,000 | 30,000 | - | - |
| LTAP/OD @ non signal | 179,000 | 108,000 | - | 71,000 |
| SCP @ non signal | 637,000 | 433,000 | - | 204,000 |
| Turn @ non signal | 45,000 | 27,000 | - | 18,000 |
| Evasive maneuver/maneuver | 12,000 | - | - | - |
| Evasive maneuver/no maneuver | 45,000 | - | - | - |
| Rollover | 6,000 | 1,000 | - | - |
| Noncollision - No impact | 36,000 | - | - | - |
| Object contacted/maneuver | 66,000 | 5,000 | - | - |
| Object contacted/no maneuver | 82,000 | 7,000 | 76,000 | - |
| Hit and run | 3,000 | - | - | - |
| Other - Rear-end | 1,000 | - | 1,000 | 1,000 |
| Other - Sideswipe | 2,000 | - | 2,000 | 2,000 |
| Other - Turn Across Path | 1,000 | 1,000 | - | - |
| Other - Turn Into Path | 1,000 | 1,000 | - | - |
| Other | 22,000 | - | - | - |
| | 5,595,000 | 1,465,000 | 3,223,000 | 3,038,000 |

**Table C2.** Target Light-Vehicle Crash Data for V2I Systems as Primary Countermeasure

| Pre-Crash Scenario | All Crashes | V2I | AV | V2V |
|---|---|---|---|---|
| No driver present | 1,000 | - | - | - |
| Vehicle failure | 45,000 | - | 45,000 | - |
| Control loss/vehicle action | 89,000 | 55,000 | - | 34,000 |
| Control loss/no vehicle action | 414,000 | 238,000 | - | 176,000 |
| Running red light | 226,000 | 226,000 | - | - |
| Running stop sign | 42,000 | 42,000 | - | - |
| Road edge departure/maneuver | 54,000 | 9,000 | - | - |
| Road edge departure/no maneuver | 240,000 | 48,000 | 192,000 | - |
| Road edge departure/backing | 68,000 | - | 68,000 | - |
| Animal/maneuver | 15,000 | - | 15,000 | - |
| Animal/no maneuver | 285,000 | - | 285,000 | - |
| Pedestrian/maneuver | 19,000 | 8,000 | 11,000 | - |
| Pedestrian/no maneuver | 39,000 | 5,000 | 35,000 | - |
| Cyclist/maneuver | 20,000 | - | 20,000 | - |
| Cyclist/no maneuver | 27,000 | - | 27,000 | - |
| Backing into vehicle | 127,000 | - | - | 127,000 |
| Turning/same direction | 195,000 | - | 195,000 | 195,000 |
| Parking/same direction | 38,000 | - | 38,000 | 38,000 |
| Changing lanes/same direction | 329,000 | - | 329,000 | 329,000 |
| Drifting/same lane | 102,000 | - | 102,000 | 102,000 |
| Opposite direction/maneuver | 9,000 | - | - | 9,000 |
| Opposite direction/no maneuver | 102,000 | - | 102,000 | 102,000 |
| Rear-end/striking maneuver | 80,000 | - | 80,000 | 80,000 |
| Rear-end/LVA | 22,000 | - | 22,000 | 22,000 |
| Rear-end/LVM | 190,000 | - | 190,000 | 190,000 |
| Rear-end/LVD | 384,000 | - | 384,000 | 384,000 |
| Rear-end/LVS | 906,000 | - | 906,000 | 906,000 |
| LTAP/OD @ signal | 195,000 | 195,000 | - | - |
| Turn right @ signal | 29,000 | 29,000 | - | - |
| LTAP/OD @ non signal | 178,000 | 108,000 | - | 70,000 |
| SCP @ non signal | 634,000 | 432,000 | - | 202,000 |
| Turn @ non signal | 43,000 | 26,000 | - | 16,000 |
| Evasive maneuver/maneuver | 12,000 | - | - | - |
| Evasive maneuver/no maneuver | 43,000 | - | - | - |
| Rollover | 3,000 | 1,000 | - | - |
| Noncollision - No impact | 30,000 | - | - | - |
| Object contacted/maneuver | 32,000 | 3,000 | - | - |
| Object contacted/no maneuver | 61,000 | 5,000 | 56,000 | - |
| Hit and run | 3,000 | - | - | - |
| Other - Rear-end | 1,000 | - | 1,000 | 1,000 |
| Other - Sideswipe | 2,000 | - | 2,000 | 2,000 |
| Other - Turn Across Path | 1,000 | 1,000 | - | - |
| Other - Turn Into Path | 1,000 | 1,000 | - | - |
| Other | 21,000 | - | - | - |
| | 5,356,000 | 1,431,000 | 3,105,000 | 2,986,000 |

**Table C3.** Target Heavy-Truck Crash Data for V2I Systems as Primary Countermeasure

| Pre-Crash Scenario | All Crashes | V2I | AV | V2V |
|---|---|---|---|---|
| No driver present | - | - | - | - |
| Vehicle failure | 5,000 | - | 5,000 | - |
| Control loss/vehicle action | 5,000 | 3,000 | - | 2,000 |
| Control loss/no vehicle action | 16,000 | 9,000 | - | 7,000 |
| Running red light | 9,000 | 9,000 | - | - |
| Running stop sign | 2,000 | 2,000 | - | - |
| Road edge departure/maneuver | 14,000 | 1,000 | - | - |
| Road edge departure/no maneuver | 17,000 | 2,000 | 15,000 | - |
| Road edge departure/backing | 8,000 | - | 8,000 | - |
| Animal/maneuver | 2,000 | - | 2,000 | - |
| Animal/no maneuver | 5,000 | - | 5,000 | - |
| Pedestrian/maneuver | 1,000 | - | - | - |
| Pedestrian/no maneuver | 1,000 | - | - | - |
| Cyclist/maneuver | - | - | - | - |
| Cyclist/no maneuver | - | - | - | - |
| Backing into vehicle | 19,000 | - | - | 19,000 |
| Turning/same direction | 28,000 | - | 28,000 | 28,000 |
| Parking/same direction | 3,000 | - | 3,000 | 3,000 |
| Changing lanes/same direction | 49,000 | - | 49,000 | 49,000 |
| Drifting/same lane | 20,000 | - | 20,000 | 20,000 |
| Opposite direction/maneuver | 1,000 | - | - | 1,000 |
| Opposite direction/no maneuver | 13,000 | - | 13,000 | 13,000 |
| Rear-end/striking maneuver | 4,000 | - | 4,000 | 4,000 |
| Rear-end/LVA | 1,000 | - | 1,000 | 1,000 |
| Rear-end/LVM | 13,000 | - | 13,000 | 13,000 |
| Rear-end/LVD | 17,000 | - | 17,000 | 17,000 |
| Rear-end/LVS | 29,000 | - | 29,000 | 29,000 |
| LTAP/OD @ signal | 5,000 | 5,000 | - | - |
| Turn right @ signal | 3,000 | 3,000 | - | - |
| LTAP/OD @ non signal | 5,000 | 3,000 | - | 2,000 |
| SCP @ non signal | 22,000 | 15,000 | - | 7,000 |
| Turn @ non signal | 5,000 | 3,000 | - | 2,000 |
| Evasive maneuver/maneuver | 1,000 | - | - | - |
| Evasive maneuver/no maneuver | 3,000 | - | - | - |
| Rollover | 1,000 | - | - | - |
| Noncollision - No impact | 11,000 | - | - | - |
| Object contacted/maneuver | 19,000 | 1,000 | - | - |
| Object contacted/no maneuver | 17,000 | 1,000 | 16,000 | - |
| Hit and run | 1,000 | - | - | - |
| Other - Rear-end | - | - | - | - |
| Other - Sideswipe | - | - | - | - |
| Other - Turn Across Path | - | - | - | - |
| Other - Turn Into Path | - | - | - | - |
| Other | 3,000 | - | - | - |
|  | 375,000 | 55,000 | 229,000 | 217,000 |

38

# Appendix D. Distribution of Pre-Crash Scenario by System Category–Combined V2V and V2I System Primary

**Table D1.** Target All-Vehicle Crash Data for Combined V2V and V2I Systems as Primary Countermeasure

| Pre-Crash Scenario | All Crashes | V2V & V2I | AV |
|---|---|---|---|
| No driver present | 1,000 | - | - |
| Vehicle failure | 50,000 | - | 50,000 |
| Control loss/vehicle action | 97,000 | 97,000 | - |
| Control loss/no vehicle action | 442,000 | 442,000 | - |
| Running red light | 226,000 | 226,000 | - |
| Running stop sign | 42,000 | 42,000 | - |
| Road edge departure/maneuver | 74,000 | 10,000 | - |
| Road edge departure/no maneuver | 277,000 | 54,000 | 223,000 |
| Road edge departure/backing | 82,000 | - | 82,000 |
| Animal/maneuver | 18,000 | - | 18,000 |
| Animal/no maneuver | 296,000 | - | 296,000 |
| Pedestrian/maneuver | 21,000 | 8,000 | 13,000 |
| Pedestrian/no maneuver | 42,000 | 5,000 | 37,000 |
| Cyclist/maneuver | 21,000 | - | 21,000 |
| Cyclist/no maneuver | 29,000 | - | 29,000 |
| Backing into vehicle | 129,000 | 129,000 | - |
| Turning/same direction | 197,000 | 197,000 | - |
| Parking/same direction | 38,000 | 38,000 | - |
| Changing lanes/same direction | 334,000 | 334,000 | - |
| Drifting/same lane | 105,000 | 105,000 | - |
| Opposite direction/maneuver | 9,000 | 9,000 | - |
| Opposite direction/no maneuver | 108,000 | 108,000 | - |
| Rear-end/striking maneuver | 81,000 | 81,000 | - |
| Rear-end/LVA | 22,000 | 22,000 | - |
| Rear-end/LVM | 192,000 | 192,000 | - |
| Rear-end/LVD | 388,000 | 388,000 | - |
| Rear-end/LVS | 910,000 | 910,000 | - |
| LTAP/OD @ signal | 195,000 | 195,000 | - |
| Turn right @ signal | 30,000 | 30,000 | - |
| LTAP/OD @ non signal | 179,000 | 179,000 | - |
| SCP @ non signal | 637,000 | 637,000 | - |
| Turn @ non signal | 45,000 | 45,000 | - |
| Evasive maneuver/maneuver | 12,000 | - | - |
| Evasive maneuver/no maneuver | 45,000 | - | - |
| Rollover | 6,000 | 1,000 | - |
| Noncollision - No impact | 36,000 | - | - |
| Object contacted/maneuver | 66,000 | 5,000 | - |
| Object contacted/no maneuver | 82,000 | 7,000 | 76,000 |
| Hit and run | 3,000 | - | - |
| Other - Rear-end | 1,000 | 1,000 | - |
| Other - Sideswipe | 2,000 | 2,000 | - |
| Other - Turn Across Path | 1,000 | 1,000 | - |
| Other - Turn Into Path | 1,000 | 1,000 | - |
| Other | 22,000 | - | - |
| | 5,595,000 | 4,503,000 | 844,000 |

**Table D2.** Target Light-Vehicle Crash Data for Combined V2V and V2I Systems as Primary Countermeasure

| Pre-Crash Scenario | All Crashes | V2V & V2I | AV |
|---|---|---|---|
| No driver present | 1,000 | - | - |
| Vehicle failure | 45,000 | - | 45,000 |
| Control loss/vehicle action | 89,000 | 89,000 | - |
| Control loss/no vehicle action | 414,000 | 414,000 | - |
| Running red light | 226,000 | 226,000 | - |
| Running stop sign | 42,000 | 42,000 | - |
| Road edge departure/maneuver | 54,000 | 9,000 | - |
| Road edge departure/no maneuver | 240,000 | 48,000 | 192,000 |
| Road edge departure/backing | 68,000 | - | 68,000 |
| Animal/maneuver | 15,000 | - | 15,000 |
| Animal/no maneuver | 285,000 | - | 285,000 |
| Pedestrian/maneuver | 19,000 | 8,000 | 11,000 |
| Pedestrian/no maneuver | 39,000 | 5,000 | 35,000 |
| Cyclist/maneuver | 20,000 | - | 20,000 |
| Cyclist/no maneuver | 27,000 | - | 27,000 |
| Backing into vehicle | 127,000 | 127,000 | - |
| Turning/same direction | 195,000 | 195,000 | - |
| Parking/same direction | 38,000 | 38,000 | - |
| Changing lanes/same direction | 329,000 | 329,000 | - |
| Drifting/same lane | 102,000 | 102,000 | - |
| Opposite direction/maneuver | 9,000 | 9,000 | - |
| Opposite direction/no maneuver | 102,000 | 102,000 | - |
| Rear-end/striking maneuver | 80,000 | 80,000 | - |
| Rear-end/LVA | 22,000 | 22,000 | - |
| Rear-end/LVM | 190,000 | 190,000 | - |
| Rear-end/LVD | 384,000 | 384,000 | - |
| Rear-end/LVS | 906,000 | 906,000 | - |
| LTAP/OD @ signal | 195,000 | 195,000 | - |
| Turn right @ signal | 29,000 | 29,000 | - |
| LTAP/OD @ non signal | 178,000 | 178,000 | - |
| SCP @ non signal | 634,000 | 634,000 | - |
| Turn @ non signal | 43,000 | 43,000 | - |
| Evasive maneuver/maneuver | 12,000 | - | - |
| Evasive maneuver/no maneuver | 43,000 | - | - |
| Rollover | 3,000 | 1,000 | - |
| Noncollision - No impact | 30,000 | - | - |
| Object contacted/maneuver | 32,000 | 3,000 | - |
| Object contacted/no maneuver | 61,000 | 5,000 | 56,000 |
| Hit and run | 3,000 | - | - |
| Other - Rear-end | 1,000 | 1,000 | - |
| Other - Sideswipe | 2,000 | 2,000 | - |
| Other - Turn Across Path | 1,000 | 1,000 | - |
| Other - Turn Into Path | 1,000 | 1,000 | - |
| Other | 21,000 | - | - |
|  | 5,356,000 | 4,417,000 | 754,000 |

40

**Table D3.** Target Heavy-Truck Crash Data for Combined V2V and V2I Systems as Primary Countermeasure

| Pre-Crash Scenario | All Crashes | V2V & V2I | AV |
|---|---|---|---|
| No driver present | - | - | - |
| Vehicle failure | 5,000 | - | 5,000 |
| Control loss/vehicle action | 5,000 | 5,000 | - |
| Control loss/no vehicle action | 16,000 | 16,000 | - |
| Running red light | 9,000 | 9,000 | - |
| Running stop sign | 2,000 | 2,000 | - |
| Road edge departure/maneuver | 14,000 | 1,000 | - |
| Road edge departure/no maneuver | 17,000 | 2,000 | 15,000 |
| Road edge departure/backing | 8,000 | - | 8,000 |
| Animal/maneuver | 2,000 | - | 2,000 |
| Animal/no maneuver | 5,000 | - | 5,000 |
| Pedestrian/maneuver | 1,000 | - | - |
| Pedestrian/no maneuver | 1,000 | - | - |
| Cyclist/maneuver | - | - | - |
| Cyclist/no maneuver | - | - | - |
| Backing into vehicle | 19,000 | 19,000 | - |
| Turning/same direction | 28,000 | 28,000 | - |
| Parking/same direction | 3,000 | 3,000 | - |
| Changing lanes/same direction | 49,000 | 49,000 | - |
| Drifting/same lane | 20,000 | 20,000 | - |
| Opposite direction/maneuver | 1,000 | 1,000 | - |
| Opposite direction/no maneuver | 13,000 | 13,000 | - |
| Rear-end/striking maneuver | 4,000 | 4,000 | - |
| Rear-end/LVA | 1,000 | 1,000 | - |
| Rear-end/LVM | 13,000 | 13,000 | - |
| Rear-end/LVD | 17,000 | 17,000 | - |
| Rear-end/LVS | 29,000 | 29,000 | - |
| LTAP/OD @ signal | 5,000 | 5,000 | - |
| Turn right @ signal | 3,000 | 3,000 | - |
| LTAP/OD @ non signal | 5,000 | 5,000 | - |
| SCP @ non signal | 22,000 | 22,000 | - |
| Turn @ non signal | 5,000 | 5,000 | - |
| Evasive maneuver/maneuver | 1,000 | - | - |
| Evasive maneuver/no maneuver | 3,000 | - | - |
| Rollover | 1,000 | - | - |
| Noncollision - No impact | 11,000 | - | - |
| Object contacted/maneuver | 19,000 | 1,000 | - |
| Object contacted/no maneuver | 17,000 | 1,000 | 16,000 |
| Hit and run | 1,000 | - | - |
| Other - Rear-end | - | - | - |
| Other - Sideswipe | - | - | - |
| Other - Turn Across Path | - | - | - |
| Other - Turn Into Path | - | - | - |
| Other | 3,000 | - | - |
|  | 375,000 | 272,000 | 52,000 |

DOT HS 811 381
October 2010

U.S. Department
of Transportation

**National Highway
Traffic Safety
Administration**

www.nhtsa.gov